Gladys Bryson.

Mar 17, 1979.

Marcus Bach

What's Right
With The World

What's Right With The World

MARCUS BACH

PRENTICE-HALL, *Inc., Englewood Cliffs, N.J.*

Printed in the United States of America

Prentice-Hall International, Inc., London
Prentice-Hall of Australia, Pty. Ltd., North Sydney
Prentice-Hall of Canada, Ltd., Toronto
Prentice-Hall of India Private Ltd., New Delhi
Prentice-Hall of Japan, Inc., Tokyo
10 9 8 7 6 5 4 3 2 1

Library of Congress Cataloging in Publication Data

Bach, Marcus,
  What's right with the world.

  1. Meditations. I. Title.
BV4832.2.B25   242   73–9623
ISBN 0–13–955096–8

Portions of this book appeared in *Unity Magazine* in somewhat different form and are
reprinted with permission.

ALSO BY MARCUS BACH:

Had You Been Born In Another Faith
Let Life Be Like This
Make It An Adventure
Strangers At The Door
The Power Of Perception
The Power Of Perfect Liberty
The Unity Way Of Life
The Will To Believe
The World Of Serendipity

*Published by Prentice-Hall

To all of those who treat the world with love and peace

Contents

What's Right
With The World

.1.

The Bridle Path

Behind my Palos Verdes home in southern California is a bridle path shaded by towering eucalyptus trees, a lane just right for an early morning walk with my schnauzer dog. Invariably we are met by a young executive who keeps in shape by jogging five miles or more at this six-thirty hour. Here he comes, trim and muscular, head high, a shock of luxuriant brown hair flapping as he runs. Hand raised in greeting, he steams past, leaving no doubt about his enthusiasm for the high adventure of another day.

One morning after he had trotted by, I noticed another young man coming slowly along the path carrying two suitcases. This fellow was a spastic, whose disoriented gait and awkward shuffle suggested that he might conceivably be experiencing pain, but he smiled and commented happily on my freshly groomed dog—who did look sharp for a change. Obviously he wanted no sympathy or help in lugging his bags to the crosswalk where he expected to be picked up by a friend.

I walked on, thinking of the contrast between this man and the jogger, when I heard a muffled thud. The spastic had stumbled and fallen headlong over his suitcases. Before I could reach his side, he was proudly back on his feet, dusting himself off, waving me away. I watched as he took a fresh, strong hold of his luggage and moved along.

Comparing these two opposites, the jogger and the handicapped, I felt a strange inexplicable rightness about a world I have never been able to decipher or explain. The impression persisted. The silent path was telling me something as if, were I to follow it even mentally, it would lead into a different and a more just world than I had ordinarily found; a world in which I might conceivably have insight into antithetical scenes of the kind I had just witnessed.

I visualized the jogger returning to his home, bolstered by his five-mile hike, the warmth of life surging through his body; I saw the spastic getting into the car content that he had been able to exercise his own control and self-reliability.

Why one man was in his situation and the other in his had not been clarified. No infallible insight had come through to me, but a hint of illumination flickered for a moment in the hazy morning shadows of the eucalyptus lane. Religion is my beat, and in my research I had often tried to figure out the complex gamut of life's strange polarities. I had engaged in speculation all the way from karmic causes, on to the sins or virtues involved in these equations, straight through to plain, unadulterated fate. Rarely had I been any wiser for it all.

By rights I should have had deeper perception into these enigmas, for I couldn't possibly have touched more lives or been touched by more personal associations in the field of faith. From intimate fellowship with sannyasin (holy men) in India to spiritual leaders in the western world; from refugees in Southeast Asia to politicians; from a renowned pianist friend who lost a hand in an accident to concert artists who seemed always to get good breaks; from sightless people with their guide dogs to physically fit Olympic stars; I had probed the reach of men's beliefs to piece together some meaningful interpretation. These people all had spiritual convictions and a philosophy to live by, but not until this moment had their voices been clear enough for me to hear not what the big world meant to them, but what went on in the micro-world, their inner world of self.

Now, for once, here in this sheltered lane, not more than a hundred steps from home, I realized that the information that friends had shared with me was much the same, no matter where they lived or who they were or what their state of life. Their contrapositions were tied together by a common network of success and longing, triumph and heartbreak, guidance and mis-guidance—even the occasional confrontation with the fear of belief in something that did not always believe in *them*. But now I sensed that these conditions did not simply run through their lives: they *were* life, this was the way life *is*. Realizing this universality and grasping its subtle ways, they found their oneness with the world and a secret comaraderie with all mankind.

In the soft sand of the familiar bridle path that early morning, the prints of both jogger and spastic were clearly defined. As I stood alone in these quiet sur-roundings not yet disturbed by the waking megalopolis, a hint of knowing dawned on me—as it surely does on every individual who for a thought-provoking moment sees himself as the center of the universe, the pinpoint of interest and reality in his micro-world, and who with breathless recognition knows that it is strictly, wholly, completely up to *him* to determine what is right for him and where he truly stands in whatever his world may be.

A perpetual myth has it that some individuals are in the special favor of the gods and some are simply pawns or puppets on a string. Belief in a chosen people and the illusion of specially favored persons have persisted since time began. Then came the mistaken theory that material blessings are heaven's most favored gift, to say nothing of other more subtle Gifts-of-the-Spirit that were often used as collateral for prestige and fame.

According to the footprints I saw, the real rightness in the world was not like that at all. It was an awareness, a sensitivity to a cosmic overlife—silent, mystic, an inner journey, a response to that something in nature which (thank God) is determined to remain beyond the hope of total finding-out.

The real rightness in the world is never obvious. At least, so I told myself as an excuse for having overlooked it for so long. Rarely is it found in the headlines and only occasionally is it hinted at by the multi-media. People who try to find it by getting-away-from-it-all usually discover that they take their troubled world with them and, after all, who wants to be a hermit? Who *could* be a hermit, for that matter, now that living space is running out? Or who, with a Calvinistic conscience, could be happy in his isolated micro-world while the macro-world is in such desperate need of understanding and repair?

I suppose everyone holds questions in his heart which he hopes time will answer. The half-secret is that we like to feel the answers will come through some sort of divine inspiration, accompanied by evidence of something more than a merely personal point of view. This was my moment. The sun, high enough to touch the silvery green of shimmering eucalyptus leaves, answered the questions for me. It zeroed in on those acquaintances in many lands who had impressed me with their incredible integrative sense; those who behind disquieting headlines kept hold of the rightness they had found and who, within the global trauma, were able to mind their dreams.

I remembered another lane, in Japan, that wound through giant cryptomeria trees. I was with a Zen Buddhist from Sojiji Temple near Tokyo. He told me about a monk, Soshi by name, who walked in quiet meditation with a companion. Passing a fish pond tucked away from the city's sounds, Soshi paused to lean over the crystal water.

"See how those fish are enjoying themselves," Soshi commented.

"How do you know they are enjoying themselves?" his companion asked. "You're not a fish."

"How do *you* know that I don't know?" came the reply. "You are not Soshi."

Surely Soshi was a right-with-the-worlder, seeing himself not as others saw him, but as he saw himself!

The people I knew in my own fullness of time proved that the stimulus of micro-world on macro-world by some yin-yang mechanism keeps things balanced and dynamic for those who catch on to the metaphysical magic. What they had been finally making clear to me, non-verbally for the most part, was that despite all outward appearances—or anything that man has done to complicate world situations, or anything fate may have effected to cause mutations in their micro-world—nothing can rob a person of his way of thinking. Which includes, of course, a way of doing and a way of knowing.

No one culture or philosophy has a corner on the formula. No religion has an exclusive on the principle.

We shape our life in the unseen before it is manifest in the seen. We fashion in the ideal what eventually appears in the real. The mind is the realm of cause; our micro-world the realm of effect.

Now, obviously, a morning walk paved by footprints in the sand, and a dog excitedly following the trail of random scents as if this were all a new terrain, makes a man reflective. He begins to wonder whether these right-with-the-worlders, these inward dreamers, might be the eventual saviors of mankind. I had speculated on this surreptitiously at times, but the macro-world was usually drumming in my ears, looking over my shoulder, pushing me, casting doubts that I could stand alone in my own cosmically centered life. The big world often talked me out of it. Now the idea seemed to be for us to start playing the game where it could be controlled, on the home court of the inner mind, in the belief that though some solutions for the macro-world were beyond reach, we could come closer to them if we recognized a quieter world within ourselves.

"What's right with the world" was not a question but an affirmation. It was a matter of the transfigured moment—memories reviewed as meaningful, serendipitous encounters seen in a new light, life holding a margin for never-ending creativity. I was already wondering how I could express the oneness I felt to other worldlings who had not been able to share their oneness verbally with me.

A psychic researcher friend of mine, Louis Anspacher, once said that the most profound responses can be told only by way of allegory. When in the folklore of the Orient someone tried to explain the miraculous, the story became Aladdin's Lamp. In ancient Greece, the discovery of ultimate good after the phasing out of the illusion of evil resulted in the legend of Pandora's Box. In medieval Europe, the alchemic secrets of the universe could be described only through the science fiction of Mephistopheles, to whom Faust sold his soul. Long ago in Galilee a Teacher gave his best advice in parables. It could be that in our day we have been too realistic and factual, and a bit too wise in our measure of true values. Perhaps whatever is right with the world can best be described as an emanation we all feel at times—the deep and knowing hint that we are never sufficiently grateful for what we have. Nor do we realize how right and necessary *both* macro- and micro-world actually are for us. This lack of gratitude may, of course, be the only thing that's really wrong.

Just now, rightness with *my* world was the scent of eucalyptus, the sight of a bridle path, a dog inquisitively waiting to see which way his master planned to go, nasturtiums hidden in the ivy and the grass, a butterfly stirring in the bougainvillea, the distant call of a peacock, the sound of a jet, the murmur of traffic, the open gateway to my home, the scent of breakfast, the sight of a loved one waiting, the vision of two men who had left their footprints in the sand.

A youngster came flashing down the lane, ambitiously pedaling his bike. His gaily spinning wheels wiped out all clues of earlier passersby and rubbed out any footmarks I had made. Bursting with life, he raised a hand as he rode by, calling out his usual greeting, "Have a good day!"

.2.

The Bridge

Forty years ago a demonstration of hypnotism was premiered in my hometown in central Wisconsin. The performance was late by about 3,000 years, considering that the art was practiced in Egypt by the priests of Isis. Late by 2,000 years if you begin with Pythagoras, or 200 years if you prefer to date the phenomenon from the Austrian physician Friedrich Mesmer.

At any rate, a hypnotist came to our village and I went with my father to see the act. When the call came for volunteers, Louie the Jeweler, a friend of ours, who was known for dabbling in the occult and the unknown, was among the first to go up stage.

The mustached and bearded hypnotist looked Louie in the eye and put him to sleep. Then he told him, "You are an athlete" (which Louie wasn't); "You have muscles like iron and a spine like steel" (which Louie hadn't); and informed him that he was now to be a living bridge—about which we of the audience had our doubts.

He placed Louie's feet on one chair and his head on another—and there was the jeweler, suspended like a catwalk without any visible support beneath his stocky 5 feet 8 inches. Then the hypnotist rested his 175 pounds on Louie's abdomen and calmly lit a cigar.

Sitting on Louie, he chatted with us about the wonders of the human mind and the need for bridges, and got up only after a series of breath-taking puffs at his cigar. Lowering Louie's legs and head from the chairs, he ordered his subject to rest, counted backwards from ten, snapped his fingers, and magically brought Louie out of it.

There were other demonstrations that night of this mysterious power tapping at the inner man, and when the show was over some townsfolk said it was the work of the devil. Others claimed it was clearly a trick. A German preacher called it *Hexerei* (witch-work).

But Louie told my father it was the beginning of a new day. Relating it to his own field, Louie explained that while most men had always studied the mechanism of watches and clocks, this bearded newcomer had familiarized himself with the tick.

When I talk with students of the youth generation these days, I often think of Louie's remark. A significant number of them are definitely more interested in the tick of life than in the mechanism of existence. The criteria which we of the "straight" generation once held about making good in the world, our creed of affluence and security, our goals of materialism and social acceptance, have lost both meaning and appeal to a sizable sector of the oncoming culture. Many of us, convinced by years of belief in the rightness of our views, find it difficult to allow any deviation from our presumptions. There is, however, a sort of hypnotic spell catching on at both the straight and the counter-culture levels which insists that the perceptive life is a bridge, has always been the bridge between generations.

I am not thinking about hypnosis now, but about insight, and have in mind serious young members of the so-called "movement" who are sincerely trying to find their way in a world that has opened new doors of perception, most of all within themselves. No longer bound by a five-sensory, four-dimensional world, they are restless and annoyed when the establishment insists on maintaining a rigid *status quo* and a belief that any digression of an alternative borders on *Hexerei.*

Some of us, however, believe that old values need not be destroyed in order for new values to be realized. Nor does perceptivity give appraisal to these values. Perceptivity *is* the value, and it is the bridge. This approach was suggested to me during a counseling session with a college student when our talk drifted into some standard academic questions: Is it possible that today's pursuits are different than they used to be, and therefore are today's directions also different? If so, where can we find a meeting of minds? What did he plan to do after he recieved his B.A. degree? What was the range of his career planning?

These questions turned him off. If he had been noncommunicative before, he was more so now. He sat on the window ledge of our campus room with weightier things on his mind.

"What do you know about *haikus?*" he challenged.

"Well, I know they are a Japanese poetic art form," I said. "In fact, a Japanese friend of mine—"

"Do you think this is a *haiku?*" he interrupted, and without so much as a glance at me, he lapsed into a reverie and began reciting half to himself:

> *The oracle spins*
> *The dreamer's dream,*
> *Plucks the lyre's theme,*
> *Gathers the sagebrush*
> *To Delphi.*

He paused, as if wondering whether he should have shared this much of himself with an off-campus lecturer whom he had met for the first time and with whom he had made an appointment on an impulse.

"I don't think so," I said.

"You don't think what?" he asked.

"I don't think it's a *haiku.*"

"No, I guess it isn't," he admitted with a shrug. "The lines aren't mine anyway. I wish they were."

I closed my eyes with a readiness to listen. He must have glanced at me or else he ESP'd my cue, because he soon continued, somewhat louder than before:

> *Whispering winds*
> *Breath,*
> *The bloom of mystic poppies*
> *Scotch broom their secrets.*
>
> *God's mischief*
> *Ventures the drama*
> *Hypnotized.*

It was sincerely and impressively done. I opened my eyes.

He stood at the window. Tall, slender, twenty. Luxuriantly long-haired, blond, as alone as if he were on the lunar surface.

"Beautiful lines," I said.

"You think so?" he asked indifferently. "Why do you say they're beautiful?"

"They say something to me," I told him.

He looked at me as if for the first time. Actually he looked beyond me—a lonely look, unconsciously dramatic.

"It could be," I explained, "that I like the lines be-

cause I was in Delphi several months ago. It had always
been my ambition to go there. The Greeks call it *Delphy,*
which is more poetic. The vapors still rise as they did
in the days of the oracle. The creek still flows as at the
time of Hadrian. I don't remember the sagebrush."

He was tempted to answer but turned his attention
instead to the ankh cross dangling on a silver cord
against his copper-colored pullover sweater. He studied the cross as if the cross were studying him.

"The Scotch broom," I went on, "is something else
that drew me to the lines. I live among Scotch broom
every summer in British Columbia. It's soft yellow.
There are also other shades. I saw it in the New Zealand
countryside. It was gold-yellow there, acres of it in the
South Island. The golden broom and the gorse."

Gradually it seemed to dawn on him that I was in the
room. When he spoke, his words were refreshingly
direct:

"Ever try writing poetry?"

"*Haiku?*"

"Any kind," he said with a shrug.

"Why do you ask?"

"Just wondered." There was a note of withdrawal in
his voice. He turned the cross over in his hands.

"To tell the truth," I told him, "when I was fifteen
I wrote a poetic diatribe against my mother and dad."

He looked at me inquiringly.

"They insisted that I work in a bank," I explained,
"which I did and which I hated, but they wanted me to
learn about security and a place in life. I didn't give a
damn about security in those days. I wanted to be a
violinist. So I wrote a poem about parental oppression,
and the despotism of the establishment, and the tyr-
anny of my uncles who owned the bank."

"Did your parents ever see the poem?"

"I laid it on the kitchen table. Of course they saw it."

"What did they say?"

"My father said it didn't rhyme," I recalled. "I think I was ahead of my time."

He started to smile but refrained, as though he felt it would have been too great a concession.

"What did your mother say?"

"She said she once wrote a poem against *her* parents. In German. She thought it was better than mine. Then she baked me a cake."

He studied me as if deciding whether I was putting him on. I wasn't, but I let him wonder. I had my own right to a reverie. Among other things I was going back through the years to Louie the Jeweler. I found myself looking out across the campus as the student had done, and quoting his lines more to myself than to him:

> *God's mischief*
> *Ventures the drama*
> *Hypnotized.*

Suddenly he was talking. "Did you ever get to be a violinist? Did you keep on at the bank? How did *you* work it out?"

"I didn't," I confessed. "It worked itself out."

His voice was eager. A wall of resistance had come down. "What do you mean, *it* worked out?"

"It worked out," I repeated with a shrug. "I won't make it sound easy. It isn't easy. Well, yes, it is. There is a world, a hidden world, a hidden meaning, a poetic meaning in life. The more we catch on and trust the meaning—Delphi, sagebrush, Scotch broom—the more it comes into our lives and gives direction."

I could sense that he was reaching for the mental switch to turn me off. "Don't give me a religious rap," he warned.

"I'm not," I answered. "I'm talking about God's mischief."

He got the message, not of something said, but of something felt. I felt it, too. We had bypassed the conventional, verbal channel of communication. He knew this and I knew it, and only the admission that we knew would have spoiled it for both of us.

"I quit the bank," I reminisced. "I left home and tried to be a violinist. Tried hard but never made it. I got to see and appreciate my parent's point of view. I never agreed with it all. They got to see mine, and they never agreed with all of mine either. But our worlds got into focus. There's a value judgment when you are fifteen, another when you're twenty, another at twenty-five, thirty, forty, and so on. If fifteen can't learn from thirty, or thirty from fifteen, if twenty can't benefit from forty, or forty from twenty, that's as bad as history not learning from the past or the past failing to foresee the future."

He placed a chair so that he could sit down and put his feet on the window ledge.

"Mind?" he said. He must have known I wouldn't mind no matter where he wanted to sit, but I was glad he asked—for reasons known only to the vestigial hangups of the establishment.

He made himself comfortable. "If you are saying that you can put yourself in my place because you were there when you were my age," he began, "and that I can put myself in your place because someday I will be where you are, that may be true. But my mom and dad broke it off five years ago. I've been the only real link they have had. I stand somewhere in between them. In between everything."

Having gone this far, he was now comfortable with our relationship. So was I.

"I'd really like to level with you," he said. "Do you have time?"

There are times that know no time, neither sidereal nor Greenwich, and that is how I felt about talking with him. What's more, there are topics so pandemic that everyone finds himself a traveler with every other person on the way. It is not a matter of having time. Time has you.

So we had our rap session about things that students are eager to talk about on campuses everywhere—subjects ranging from the peer generation to war and peace, from God to man and his environment, from sex and racism and violence to law-and-order, from death and dying to life-to-come, from license to love. Such sessions are not prearranged or scheduled. They happen. I don't know what we settled as far as resolving any great issues goes, but at least we learned that the highest good begins not only with things said but also with responses deeply felt.

When I realized how fast the hours had gone and how much the student and I had in common although we lived on relatively different time-tracks of existence, I remembered Louie and the bridge. Louie, in his time, had a way of connecting worlds in transition. There were gaps between generations in those days, and there were many people who thought in terms of tricks and witches. Louie was interested in the tick of life.

As I recalled Louie, I was already wondering whether there might someday be a mature and balanced man recalling a day when, as a student, he took his feet down from a window ledge and pressed the hand of an off-campus visitor with whom he had talked awhile, not merely about items on the customary agenda, but about Delphi and the oracle, whispering winds and breath, Scotch broom, sagebrush and the dreamer's dream. Better still, of how

> *God's mischief*
> *Ventures the drama*
> *Hypnotized.*

Come to think of it, there must be something right with a world like this.

.3.

The Swallows

I was at the Old Mission when the swallows came back to Capistrano. It was March 19, St. Joseph's Day. The California sun was sending its first layers of light across the ancient chapel walls when I caught sight of glistening wings above the morning sky. Excited cries went up from a group of young people who had waited out the night on blankets and in cars.

"There they are! They've come three thousand miles! Hey, those are the scouts; the main flock will be along later!"

The white pigeons on the Mission grounds fluttered as if to remind us swallow-watchers that they too deserved attention. But our eyes were focused on the dozen or more small, violet-green birds, their white throats shining, their swallowtail coats smartly pressed, returning obediently at the appointed time as if a cosmic clock had alerted them and a cosmic radar had guided them unerringly on their pattern of flight.

The teeming freeways, the vast Pacific, the winds, the smog, a recent earthquake—nothing had detoured or deterred them. They were returning to their summer home at the Mission of San Juan Capistrano, which lies beside the traffic lanes between Laguna Beach and San Clemente in the Golden State.

We who watched saw something remarkably right

with the world in the phenomenon of the swallows' return. How reassuring to find that there are still those who keep their promises, who can be depended upon, who set a date and keep it! But more than that, how right the world when rhythm and harmony are established between life and the universe! How wonderful to think that there are those, whether they be birds or human beings, who make use of both favorable and unfavorable winds, knowing how to stay on course and how to live at oneness with some stellar plan!

I had witnessed this before, some twenty years ago. At that time it was a cold, damp morning that found me standing there on the Mission grounds on St. Joseph's Day. I was greatly moved when I learned (be it legend or fact) that the birds had returned each year on March 19, come rain or shine, ever since the Mission was founded in 1776. Twenty years ago I had thought about *their* relationship with the Unseen. Now I thought about *mine,* my flight pattern, how *I* am guided and directed and often moved in paths beyond my knowing. For once my thoughts were turned not outward but within. I was the bird who was coming home.

Someone once said that swallows spurn the earth, preferring to live in "the lucid interspace of world and world." This could be a vital secret in discovering the rightness about things—to be in the world and not of it, and yet to have the courage and the will to fly intimately into the mystery and wonder of existence.

Several of the swallows swooped down. I held my breath in expectation as one of the more adventurous ones balanced himself on a wire and looked down at me as if to say, "Where did you spend the winter? What has happened to you since a year ago? How do things look through your eyes?"

Actually he may not have had me in mind at all. He may already have been contemplating a building site, a slab of wall on the belfry perhaps, a place with a view—just right for the home of clay and spittle he would soon be ingeniously constructing. Or perhaps he was wondering whether we mortals appreciated the fact that we too were now capable of flying from South America and feeding on the wing as he had done. He flew only by day, but we could keep on going day and night at a speed never dreamed of by our feathered friends.

Yet all of this was beyond man's wildest hopes in 1776. We earthlings certainly had made progress when you stopped to think about it. Swallows were still flying as they always had, building their nests of mud and straw just as their ancestors had done, traveling the same routes, using sheer bird-power without any special innovations.

Considered in this light, who could doubt the marvel and wonder of man and his amazing world? Think how he has evolved and progressed. Picture the burdens he used to carry on his back, the weary footsore treks he used to make, the sweat and toil with which he had to buy his daily bread, the limited sphere of his neighborhood before he learned how to transport himself, communicate, and tap the resources of his world!

When I thought of the automobiles and the planes that had brought these crowds to Capistrano just to welcome a flock of swallows, the affluence of our life was overwhelming. In each home represented you could imagine a TV or two, and radios, and refrigerators, running water, warmth, and food in abundance. Everything in comfort and in style. Everything taken as a matter of course.

This ability of man's to evolve, to seize the raw ideas of the universe and materialize them, to investigate and explore, to continually change and improve his world, was no doubt his most notable distinction. No other species or subspecies, genus or subgenus had such capabilities or demonstrated such amazing power and limitless skill. The Psalmist was dead right when he extolled man's greatness and reminded God that:

> . . . *Thou hast made him a little lower than the angels, and has crowned him with glory and honour.*
> *Thou madest him to have dominion over the works of thy hands; thou hast put all* things *under his feet:*
> *All sheep and oxen, yea, and the beasts of the field;*
> *The fowl of the air* [and this surely included cliff swallows], *and the fish of the sea, and whatsoever passeth through the paths of the seas . . .*

Such a work is man! We knew it and we were not letting God forget it. But when I sent these thoughts in the direction of the lone swallow balanced adroitly on the wire, he was gone in a flash. He took off in a split second. No warming up of the engines, no runway, no adjusting of goggles or fastening of seat belt, He was off and out of sight in the blink of an eye.

It was all very well to look back at what man had achieved and to rest on our scientific laurels. We were surely justified to sing the Psalmist's song or to relive our landing on the moon, or to tune in on channel Telstar. Where was the swallow who could match those miracles? But in looking backward on what man had done, I got to thinking of what was *left* for man to do and what the next most needed field of creativity seemed to be.

In short, I got to thinking about celestial navigation.

How *did* the swallows make their flight if not by some cosmic orientation which still defies the reach of man? Is their secret based on sight or smell or sound beyond our knowing, or on some psychic telemetry that no living mortal has ever figured out?

How do ducks know when to migrate and how far to travel north or south or how to hold their course when they brave the powerful ocean passage to Hawaii? How does the Laysan albatross find its way back to its habitat after being carted by man a thousand miles from home? Do robins wait for spring, or is it the other way around? How does the tern find its way from arctic to antarctic and back again? What guides the sanderling from Patagonia to the Great Northwest? How does the hummingbird find its way, flying at fifty miles an hour through the dead of night?

One thing is sure: something in the universe is cosmically related to something in the bird. It must be as simple and as profound as that. There is a rightness somewhere, a oneness with the creative Power which brought the creature into being.

As if to confirm the rightness, a swallow again made a perfect landing on the wire. Its tiny buttercup beak trembled in nervous motion as if telling us it was much too busy to acknowledge an elaborate welcome.

"Don't you know," it argued, "I'll be here only until October 23rd, and then I'll leave as punctually as I came?"

Watching it on its perch above the Mission's aging stones, I thought of Tennyson's reflections on the flower in the crannied wall:

I hold you here, root and all, in my hand,
Little flower—but if I could understand

What you are, root and all, and all in all,
I should know what God and man is.

That the bird was an expert in aerodynamics went
without saying. But where had he gone to school? Who
awarded him his degree? For maneuverability and
"aerobatics" he was decidedly more adept than man,
but who had taught him the techniques? And the question was, how did he follow his flight pattern without
charts or instruments and without a navigator at his
side? Were these all standard equipment, neatly packaged inside his featherweight brain? Did he, I wondered, instinctively know that the earth is rotating and
that the heavenly bodies, with the exception of the
North Star, change their positions in relation to our
whirling earth? Who programmed him? What multi-
million-dollar corporation designed his computer system and stored it in his dime-sized head?

A naturalist who stopped in at our British Columbia
cabin one evening when Canadian geese were gaily
honking in the moonlight during their migratory flight,
insisted that they hold to their course by the North Star
and that these flocks, flying in precise formation, trust
their leader to guide them on the turns and necessary
alterations in their unerring route.

Celestial navigation, I told myself on that morning
in Capistrano, is definitely what we need. It is not only
"for the birds," it is for man. It means traveling not by
the stars alone, but being in harmony with the universe
and responding to our own coded inner impulse to
trust what we call God's will and God's direction for our
lives.

The fact is, anyone who does *not* learn celestial navigation can hardly find his way around these days. He

can scarcely keep on course in the kind of world that man has made. He needs something to steer by. The rightness about it all is that "the stars are still there" —God's changeless rules to live by and His signs to fly by are still valid: love, compassion, the awareness within ourselves that we are guided, governed and guarded by God's power and His particularization in us.

I looked at it this way. The days when the swallows return to Capistrano are festive days. There are parades and hawkers and marching bands and ice-cream vendors. There are occasional street brawls; there is raucous fun. Some people romanticize and sentimentalize the occasion. Others make a pretense of debunking the entire affair. The swallows aren't really swallows, they say; they are sweeps or swifts. But whatever they are they should be banned because of the messy way they build their nests and the "pollution" they leave behind.

Anything that is said about birds can be said about people. You get the feeling that Capistrano is a miniature world where everyone comes to see a miracle and remains to eat, drink and be merry, and then write home about it. During the swallow advent period the town is definitely a picture of the world at large. Your world, my world. Everyman's world. A world with an historic Old Mission as the center of man's faith.

You walk amid the festivity and you discover people with thoughts as deep as your own, deeper thoughts than those indicated by hot dogs and taffy candy twirled on sticks. You begin to realize that you yourself are a "miracle" guided and inspirited by a life greater than your own, sustained by a creative power higher than your own, touched by a sense of wonder and compassion beyond the reaches of your own. You have a hunch that many a swallow in its long and wearying flight often wonders, as you do, whether others have their moments of doubt and faith about the rightness of the world, and you check your flight pattern and spread your wings with hope—and somehow make it to the church on time.

For a moment you are a pilot versed in celestial navigation. Everything fits ingeniously in place. Past, present and future are one. You wander away by yourself, trusting your guidance. You walk the Mission cloister or stroll the beach or stay among the jostling crowds. It does not matter. All is well. The swallows have come back once more to Capistrano.

.4.

The Lens

Few surroundings are lonelier than a deserted movie theatre. This was particularly true on a rainy Monday morning as I walked with a theatre manager through his half-dark movie house and up a ramp to the projection room suspended above the balcony. Here was an equally lonely scene: two motion picture projectors in danger of being junked because of changing times.

This period, several years ago, was the time of transition, when the czars of the cinema had readied the public for super-spectacular, bigger-than-life images —even if it meant the old army of projectors had to go. The wide screen had come to town. Cinemascope was in the making. The wide-angle view was wider than the standard projector had bargained for. Had these machines been human, they would have protested and applied for government assistance, or accepted the inevitable fate of being carted away to a metal morgue.

What chased the gloom away and made me feel there was something still right with the world was the fact that these projectors in movieland across the country were actually to have a new lease on life, thanks to the ingenuity of men in Europe and America who had pooled their creative skills and fashioned a new lens, an amazing anamorphic lens sufficiently versatile to convert the standard machines into efficient instruments which could once more serve the onward-going world of make-believe.

I often thought about the magic of the anamorphic lens as the screens grew ever larger and as the curved screen and the wrap-around screen made their advent. But the point of it all became most graphic the other day when a senior citizen came into my office for a counseling session.

He informed me with a sigh that he was deep in the throes of what the doctors had termed a "retirement syndrome." This, he had been told, was a condition brought about by displacement from established security, change in life, psychosis of environmental shock, fantasies of rejection, and so on. Since the diagnosis had cost him a tidy sum, I could see he was not about to write it off until he got his money's worth, in attention at least.

Usually when people saw his disconsolate look, his trembling hands, his shortness of breath, they were moved to ask, "What's wrong?"

This was his cue. "Retirement syndrome," he would say with authority. "It hits you all at once, or it can hit you gradually." He usually followed this by a series of medical statistics and pathological phrases straight from the doctor's mouth.

I could not tell him he looked bad because, never having seen him before, I had no idea how he should look. He had just moved to Southern California from the Midwest.

"How do you think I look?" he asked.

"You look fine to me."

He shook his head.

"I may look that way," he admitted sadly, "but how

about this?" He held out a hand. It trembled. "Feel it in my legs, too," he said, as if disappointed that he could not show me assuring evidence of the fact.

He had been a successful tailor, highly respected until the tailoring business tapered off and men apparently no longer needed his professional services. Those were changing times. So he reminisced:

"Even the governors of Iowa used to come to me for their suits. Those were the days you could tell about a man just by looking at what he wore. You can't do that any more. Not only here in California—it's the same wherever you go. It's not only the youngsters. It's everybody. It's the way of the world."

Twelve years ago, after having given up his private business, he became the tailor in a men's ready-to-wear.

"I used to take my customers into consideration when I had my own business. We used to talk things over. None of that in the men's store. The salesmen buzzed for me. I had to say a suit looked good on a man even if it looked lousy. Sell, sell. You had to sell. And the prices! Everything has changed!"

So he and his wife came to California where a son lived and where, they had been assured, the weather was always perfect. Furthermore, there was Governor Reagan.

"He's from Iowa, you know. I often used to listen to Ron Reagan's broadcasts in my tailor shop."

He had been impressed by reports that Reagan had promised to do something about smog and pollution and taxes and the hippies in California. These conditions still existed. Now, after seven months, the man who had put aside his needle and thread missed the change of seasons as much as he did tailoring, and Reagan couldn't do anything about that. He was also

haunted by the bigness of L.A. and the impersonaliza-
tion of it all.

"The other day I tried to buy some stick matches. Did
you ever try that? Where do you go to get a spool of
thread or a button? Have you tried to buy a button
lately?"

Worst of all, he confided, was the loneliness. He
could not even share the depth of this with his wife. The
awful loneliness, the sense of not being needed or
wanted.

"Back home I'd walk down the street and somebody
always knew me or I ran into somebody I knew. Somebody needed me. Even in the men's shop, bad as it was,
at least I was needed."

It occurred to him that he had even been needed
around the house, back in his Iowa home. There were
things to fix and a garden to look after and a lawn to
tend. Now they lived in an apartment on the seventh
floor. Everything was taken care of. He used to think
it would be wonderful to have everything taken care of.
Instead, it was awful.

"Seven months and all I've had to do is change a light
bulb. Something goes wrong with the toilet or the dish-
washer or the thermostat, don't touch it! We don't
know half a dozen people in the whole building. The
phone hardly ever rings. I was glad to hear it ring one
day even if it was only the L.A. *Times* wanting to know
if we didn't want the Sunday paper delivered to the
door."

He was sure he shouldn't have left the Midwest, but
he would never go back, just on general principles.
What should he do? "Look at me shake!" And he held
out trembling hands.

I took his hands in mine. They were surprisingly

warm. We rested our clasped hands on the desk as we sat opposite each other, and just as I was formulating some approach to his problem, as luck would have it the telephone rang.

Reaching for the receiver I said jokingly, "Probably the L.A. *Times*."

He tried to smile.

It wasn't the *Times*, but my visitor's wife wanting to know if he had made it to the office and was feeling okay. She wanted to remind him to start home before the peak of traffic, yet she assured me he was an excellent driver for a man of sixty-seven. He seemed more in control of himself when behind the wheel, even though he constantly complained about the freeways.

I relayed what she had said. He was pleased, but only for a moment. "If my doctor knew I drove over here all by myself—" he began.

"Once upon a time," I interrupted, "there was a movie projector . . . and it was on the verge of a retirement syndrome."

I leaned back in my chair and put my feet up on the desk. This was not my custom, but it was a sign of relaxing that also relaxed him and put him at ease. He made himself comfortable, took off his glasses, breathed on them and began to polish them thoughtfully with the white handkerchief which had been tucked properly into the pocket of his well-fitting dark suit.

"Movie projector?" he asked suspiciously, giving me a quizzical look as if wondering whether he had been right in making the appointment with me in the first place.

"Movie projector," I repeated. "It could have been in a theatre in Des Moines twelve years ago. About the time you got to wondering about your changing times."

He put on his glasses and returned his kerchief to his pocket.

"Actually," I continued, "it has to do with lenses."

I went on, developing an analogy between an anamorphic adaptor for a lens and one for a man's point of view when he finds himself confronted by an ever larger screen on which he is challenged to project his total response to life. What the lens actually does is squeeze the image on the film in the photographing process and unsqueeze it during the projection.

I felt that the comparison would be good for both my visitor and me, even though our ways of life, our "programming," our sense of being needed, were apparently completely antithetical. Nonetheless, who hasn't seen personified "projectors" with "old lenses" going to their jobs, or refusing jobs or wanting jobs, grousing about conditions, who hasn't heard them complaining that the theatre of life is no longer what it used to be, the scenes too realistic, overpowering, the music too loud, the scenes too sick, philosophies and values too distorted—that there is nothing right with the world?

But there is something right—the inner lens. The up-to-us privilege of producing pictures according to the light of the sensitized spirit in each of us. The creative point of view. The challenge rather than the threat of the wide screen. These things are right, and it did not seem out of place at this point to remind ourselves of the fact. I suggested that this was not necessarily anything new. The ancient philosopher Plotinus once said, "The eye would fail to see the sun if it were not itself a sun."

"By this," I said, "he meant that the process of seeing is a spiritual act. Carl Jung surmised that 'the eye is the maternal bosom and the pupil is its child.' That means a motherly insight when it comes to observing the world and patience with the pupil-child. A good way for us to look at the changing world."

"If you mean that adjustment to life depends on a way of looking at things," my visitor said, "I always considered myself pretty good at that."

"Looking at things *and* projecting things," I went on. "We must take both into account. On a negative film the light parts are the blackest and the black parts the brightest. All this is reversed on a positive print. Now if we think of our reactions to things in this way, it may be that as long as they are negative, we see things just reversed from what they really are."

"Could be," he agreed.

"I have a friend," I recalled, "who went through your drama of retirement syndroming. He could have said it is time to junk the old projector, but he didn't. He insisted on trying to see a rightness rather than a wrongness about the way of his world. He forced himself to look at his circumstances and his surroundings as a new show for which he needed a new lens—of understanding. So he got going. He found something to do where he felt he was needed. He retrained for another job. He went after new friends and he found them. The amazing thing was that when he changed his attitude, things began moving his way. When he stopped looking back and started looking ahead, things began to happen *through* him, like a new film passing through the anamorphic projector system."

My visitor got to thinking. He admitted that if he were to return to the Midwest, get back to where he felt he was needed, he would get over his cherished syndrome the moment he stepped on Iowa soil. In the same breath he let it be known that if he did go back, he would not be satisfied because he *was* actually ready for a "new show," an adventure in a new environment.

He confessed he had never really tried to make friends in his California surroundings and had made no effort to get involved in a project that might start his telephone ringing. Now that he thought about it, he was surprised at his lack of initiative. It wasn't like him, he said.

He was a Mason but he had never looked into the lodges in his new location. He was a Kiwanian but had not yet gone to a meeting. Nor had he and his wife done any serious research in finding a church where they might feel at home. It occurred to him that when it came to repairs, he had used the apartment rule of "Don't do it" as an excuse not to add a bit of himself to the creative plan of the apartment. As he now probed the resources of his inner self, he found it in better shape than he had imagined and he wondered why he had delayed so long in coming into his own.

"There is one thing I've often thought," he mused with a note of knowing. "Our grandchildren, seventeen and nineteen, have more ideas about changing the world than are good for them—or for the world, for that matter. This bothered me. I couldn't get *my* ideas to stick with them. Take money, for example. When I was their age I knew the value of a dollar. They think it grows on trees. Not that they're bad kids, but you wonder what's going to happen to them when they grow up."

He answered his own question by pulling himself together with sudden enthusiasm.

"I've often told myself," he said with a wave of ambition, "that if they think they can make it against my world, darned if I won't find a way to make it against theirs! Know what I mean?"

"I do and I don't," I said. "Seems to me it is a matter of making it *with* the other's world, rather than against it. And that will take a sensitive adjustment of the inner lens in both generations."

For the first time since our visit he smiled, as if he wanted the world to know he had a great many hidden potentials that nobody really knew about, as if he caught on to things a great deal quicker than I suspected. It was as if he were suddenly ready to rally his resources and get his show on the road.

After all, having been a tailor, he must have known a great deal about life styles and the cut of a man's mind.

At least a rightness about the world came through to him. Perhaps all he actually needed was someone to whom he could unburden himself. There was even a rightness, he felt, about his determination to show his wife he could drive home through the very peak of traffic as he would now have to do.

Whatever it was, a change had taken place. I was sure of this when he extended his hands to me to say good-by and I realized that they were noticeably steadier than before. Steady enough, in fact, to thread a needle, if he could but find one in the haystack called L.A.

I had the feeling that with the aid of a good lens, perhaps he could.

.5.

The
Unforgettable

In the not infrequent moments when I wonder what's right with the world, I come around to a fixed star in the whirling galaxy of life: memories.

The firm set of this star was impressed upon me when a friend of mine, feeling that the world was getting him down, decided to visit the farm home where he had spent his boyhood some thirty years ago. Now this can be a dangerous journey, and anyone who has the courage to make the trip is taking a chance. The old haunts will not be the same, nor are you the same person who once inhabited them.

Nonetheless, this fellow was determined. He got into his car and drove 1,800 miles from his Los Angeles high-rise apartment to those half-remembered acres in South Dakota.

The trip turned out to be exactly what he needed. Even though the farm bore few resemblances to the place he had known, he found intact and quite unchanged a winding creek, a grove of trees, and a wooden marker he once had placed over the grave of his pet dog, killed when it got under the wheels of the first farm truck his father had purchased. When he found this marker he also discovered a new meaning in life and a point of contact with an inner quietude that brought him back to Los Angeles a noticeably changed man.

"That collie's death," he told me, "had been one of my first and worst disillusionments. When I saw the marker on which I had tearfully etched the dog's name, I had a most wonderful sense of understanding. The unforgettable was suddenly filled with unexpected good. I walked along the creek and through the grove and felt an unbelievable nearness to God. Something told me that my life has always been in good hands."

His phrase, "the unforgettable," stayed in my mind.

"The memory," Emerson once said, "has a fine art of sifting out the pain and keeping all the joy. We remember that which we understand, and we understand best what we like. This doubles our power of attention and makes it our own."

It occurred to me that the unforgettable might actually constitute the essence of life, the extract of all that is worthwhile and precious after our experiences have been thoroughly filtered by time. The thoughtful phrase, "I remember," could be the best possible stabilizer in putting us back in balance with a basic rightness in the world.

I proved it for myself, and so can you. When frustrated or hung up on the way things are going, think back on some related scene out of the unforgettable. Instantly you are in another dimension. Immediately the affairs of the present are reassessed. You are absorbed by a new perspective, and when the flow of time resumes, it is filled with unusual meaning and depth.

I made one of my most convincing tests on the 4th of July last year. Like many another American, I had realized for some time that our traditional holidays have become little more than weekend extensions with presidential proclamations lethargically tacked on to keep up appearances. I had always been taught to be patriotically sentimental about the American Way, but the once exciting observances associated with these days had systematically gone by the board until many a cherished custom was little more than good copy for parodies and burlesque. Yet, just beneath the apparent emptiness of the old fervor, I found the magic of the unforgettable and used it to return a rightness to my world, as I am sure anyone can do no matter what his age or where he lives on the time-track of American life.

In my case, when I viewed the national scene in anticipation of the Glorious Fourth and found myself confronted mainly by casualty figures predicted for the weekend highway toll; when I again sensed the change that has taken place in our sentiment about the day's observances, I called on memory to bring back the unforgettable. Instantly a mental miracle took place.

Once more I was back in my parental home. I recalled how in that boyhood period the neighborhood, the village, the farmlands were the center of the universe. Once more the spirit of America was incorporated in the thought of "Independence Day." I remembered how, as a boy, I used to prepare for this red-letter day weeks in advance. Scraping together my nickels and dimes, I amassed an amazing assortment of firecrackers which I stashed away in cardboard cartons under my bed. What a thrill to sleep on such an arsenal! What an adventure to hoist the flag on the front porch of my home on the morning of the 4th and to command the volleys of innocent explosives that lifted tin cans tree high. What an event at night, to direct the placement and ignition of after-dark pyrotechnics which ended with sky-rockets and Roman candles vying with those of an equally festive and friendly gathering in a neighbor's yard.

Memory brought back the scene of the many times, after the 4th was over, when my mother sat next to my bed and commented on my skill as a pyrotechnician or admired my burned and blistered fingers, a fitting token of the greatness of the day. "What's the good of an adventure if there is no risk in it?" she used to say. In return, I paid my compliments to the picnic dinner she had prepared, the ice cream my father had churned, the reminiscences my uncles had recounted, until I fell asleep in the soft, white linen sheets while wisps of gunpowder drifted through the open window, provoking dreams of victory and peace.

The unforgettable. Memory, the fixed star.

Emerging from my reverie, I found the present Independence Day undergirded with new meaning. True, times have changed. To be sure, the holiday is no longer what it was. Today you can be fined for firing a cannon-cracker in your own backyard or be arrested for sending a Roman candle across your neighbor's lawn. Today it is the exception rather than the rule for relatives to gather together and recount the meaning of the day. All these are things of the past. But the unforgettable persuades us that the *spirit* of patriotism is beyond externalization. Every age is bound to express itself in its own way, in its own world setting, and according to its own distinctive pattern. Let each generation work out its own sense of values and develop its own life-style of patriotic tradition.

A Biblical proverb warns us not to remove the ancient landmarks which our fathers have set. Who are the fathers and where is the man who fails to look back upon landmarks, not necessarily of his father's, but those of his youth, no matter when he lived? What is needed most is some cherished memory stored in the heart as an unforgettable, not only in the realm of patriotism but in the total circumference of life. For if our national holidays tie us to a lively reminder of the greatness of America, consider how our religious festivals once served as the mooring for a spiritual consciousness rich with meaning and joy. This, also, can be said to be a thing of the past. Think what has happened to these "holy days"; where would we be if we had no "unforgettables" to give them balance and meaning in our runaway world?

Christmas, as everyone knows, has become the top commercial attraction of the fiscal year, a frenetic time of giving and getting. Yet Christmas, as everyone also knows, is mostly a matter of memory, and that is what keeps it great. Fortunate is he who can remember a Christmas tree with candles, a Santa Claus without a company label, and actual stockings hung by the chimney with care. Happy are those who know the old songs and sing them uncritically. But those too young to have these memories have new songs equally beautiful and other fixed stars, even the one that shone over Bethlehem which they interpret in their own way. Some will look back nostalgically on Christmases when they stood long-haired around a tree that was not even cut down, but left standing out of ecological respect, and an Advent season that shunned any gift but love and a Christmas flower. In every time and every age, what's most right with the world is the unforgettable.

All holy days are most sacred in terms of the remembered past. I have always contended that Easter is the best church-going day in the liturgical year because of a collective, unconscious awareness of immortality.

Something deep within us recalls a miracle of resurrection. Christ rising on the third day is corroboration of an event our spirit has already experienced. It is not so much a revelation as a confirmation, a remembering. At Easter one generation recalled an open sepulchre and reported seeing a Man in white whom they mistook to be the gardener. Another generation recounted the church's version of the meaning of that miracle, while another remembered the struggle to maintain the belief. The next thrilled to its discovery of the symbolism, still another to the wonder of the liturgy. Some hold as their fixed stars Easter lilies, Easter clothes, Easter eggs, the Easter parade, psychism—or relate it to the marvel of a man in space. Each unforgettable imparts its own rightness to its particular hurrying world.

Somewhere back along the way I knew an elderly woman in a little Kansas town. She had palsy and was confined for many years to a wheel chair. I have never forgotten her round and rosy face, her twinkling blue eyes, the spotlessly white dresses she wore, always with a fragile touch of color, the mellow manner she had of accepting life, as if every day were a visitor to be warmly entertained. We all knew her as Aunt Polly.

She lived in three worlds at once—past, present, and the world to come. What I remember most about her was how she handled the unforgettable, how memory sustained her and how remembering was a therapy. Reminiscences can be boring if they are overdone, and memory removed from reality becomes a falling star. Aunt Polly had a subtle way of playing it straight.

At the time when I was supplying a church in Aunt Polly's hometown of Fairview, Kansas, I was young, ambitious and full of inexperience. One of my greatest challenges was my obstreperous church choir. The con-

stant wrangling that went on made me agree with whoever it was that said a choir is the church's Pentagon—
the war department.

Things got so bad, and jealousy and temperament
ran so high, that I dropped in on Aunt Polly to unburden myself. She sat with proud dignity in her wheelchair, her silken hair dazzling white, her eyes sparkling,
her uncontrollable pale hands shaking faintly as they
rested in her lap.

As she listened patiently to my complaining, I could
feel the wheels of remembrance turning in her mind as
she replayed back more than eighty years of her affilia-
tion with the church I served. When I finished my story
she nodded understandingly.

"When I was a little girl," she reminisced, "we had
a circuit preacher, Pastor Joe, who came riding in twice
a month on his white horse, his leather-bound Bible
always ready at hand. He was a big, bearded man and
he preached powerful sermons. On the Sunday he un-
veiled our first church organ there was an awful quarrel
between two women, each wanting to be the first to play
the dedication hymn. They drew straws and that settled
that, but there was always bad blood between them.
Then the congregation took sides and it looked as if the
church would be split right down the middle."

She nodded thoughtfully as if to the monitor who was
bringing back the scene.

"One Sunday in the dead of winter," she went on,
"when Pastor Joe had driven through a snowstorm to
get here, he said he was very weary of all the bickering.
It had gotten so bad, he told the congregation, that he
was sure God would settle the organ matter in His own
way.

"God did," Aunt Polly chuckled. "On Monday morning after Pastor Joe had ridden his horse out of town, we found the organ chopped to pieces and tossed into a snowbank. And we never saw Pastor Joe again. Oh, how I loved that man!"

She laughed till tears stood in her eyes. The devoted woman who waited on her came forward dutifully with a white lace kerchief and brushed the tears away. Then she served us coffee and cookies.

Aunt Polly held her cup defiantly in her shaking hands and sipped her coffee carefully. "That is what you may have to do with your choir," she announced wistfully. "Throw them in the snow!" Then she looked me over. "No," she said appraisingly, "you are not Pastor Joe. And anyway, it's spring. You better just love them and know that God will somehow work it out."

God did. In the fall a high school music teacher came to town and managed to bring my singing members together most harmoniously.

Holidays and holy days, a church choir, an Aunt Polly in a wheelchair, or a weathered marker over a puppy's grave—something definitely right is woven in and through the pattern of life. There is the touch of a craftsman's hand in you and me, no matter how far we go astray or how unerringly we walk the line.

We can stand the rush and pace of things by returning to moments of calm. We can endure loneliness by recalling the hours when we wished with all our heart that we could be alone. Memory keeps weaving in and out of our day-by-day encounters, balancing our lives, helping us keep our bearings, steadying our sense of values, giving us the grand connection with the infinite and the eternal as if we were actually in control.

And often when I commune thoughtfully with the unforgettable, I think we are.

.6.

The Raft

MOOLOOLABA, AUSTRALIA

Four men in tattered clothes, a charcoal chip of a raft, and a cat named Minette entered Mooloolaba Harbour at 11:50 last night, ending a 7000-mile voyage across the Pacific from South America to Australia.

The report flashed across the down-under continent on November 6, 1970. It caught the world's news services, and pushed Vietnam, the Middle East, politics, crime and even the running of the Melbourne Cup from the front pages of the Australian press. A landing from outer space could not have caused more excitement than the arrival of this "charcoal chip" which, with its four intrepid men and a cat, had conquered more miles of surging surf than any raft in man's recorded history of the sea.

I was in Sydney at the time. My wife was in north Australia at the Great Barrier Reef. She telephoned to say, "The excitement here is fantastic! The men were on the raft for five months. Nobody seemed to know anything about them until they suddenly appeared out of nowhere. Are people excited about it in Sydney?"

They were. They paused in the morning sun, gazing at headlines and pictures of the four bearded adventurers standing nonchalantly on their homemade raft whose keel consisted of seven 30-foot-long balsa logs. Its open cabin was a deck-shelter of bamboo and grass, a tiny 6 by 9 foot hutch as primitive as any in the Ecuadorian bush from whose shores the launching had taken place. These invincible explorers had journeyed unaided by any form of engine power. Using only sail and current and their own indomitable will, they proved that South American Indians could conceivably have migrated to Australia by this same method ten thousand years ago.

Every phase of the expedition was dramatic. The rugged four who built and piloted the raft represented four nationalities, four countries: Vitale Alzar, twenty-three, a Spaniard; Marcel Modena, forty-three, of France; Gabriel Von Godin Salas, thirty-two, a Chilean; and twenty-five-year-old Canadian Norman Tetrault. Such was the crew aboard *La Balsa* as she sailed and drifted and bobbed and pitched across the mercurial stretches of the world's largest ocean (64 million square miles), deepest ocean (average depth 14,000 feet), and most fathomless ocean (sounded at one point to a depth of 39,000 feet).

La Balsa, a ragtag raft, on target after 165 days and nights at sea!

"We had our share of weather," Captain Alzar reported as the raft lulled in Mooloolaba Harbour. "The trip was bad sometimes. We were harnessed to the rigging when things were worst. We often fell overboard when there was work to do in a storm, but we always got back. There were beautiful days when we would swim alongside. We saw hundreds of sharks around us. Only three ships passed us in our long journey. We got nothing from them. But the raft, she was very good! *Magnifico La Balsa!*"

She *was* magnificent, though now as she rested in still

waters, she seemed a motley tangle of ropes, rigging, water casks and salt-sprayed drift. This outer appearance was deceptive. As one of the men said, "You can't see her spirit just by looking at her."

That was true. As she lay in the harbor you could hardly realize how well she had taken the storms, the calm, the days, the nights, the cold and heat, the damaging waves and the pounding rain. Her balsa logs were lashed together with hemp ropes. A mainmast supported by bamboo guys and a crosspiece and a mizzenmast affixed to the thatch-covered cabin rose proudly from the platform. Flags of many nations dangled from her rigging, and her mainsail bore a design of the sun and the planets painted by Salvador Dalí. She was a good ship, though she looked like a peasant's shack that had accidentally slid into the sea on a rainy night.

She had ridden the 7,000 miles faultlessly until, seventy miles from the Queensland Australian coast, she scraped a reef. It was irritating and frustrating to think *La Balsa* had come all that way and then had to be towed the few remaining miles into Mooloolaba. But, then, that's life!

The analogy had occurred to me as it must have to many others, but it took an incident in a King's Cross coffee house to make it unforgettable. On the day following the arrival of the raft, I was having a *cappucino* (exotic expresso-style coffee) at one of the small round tables with the *La Balsa* news-story propped up in front of me. The place was fairly crowded, so I was not unduly surprised when a stranger pulled up a chair and set his fragrantly steaming *cappucino* cup near mine. My new tablemate was a long-haired, college-age American who gave me a cordial look when he realized how engrossed I was in the voyagers' account.

"Magnifico La Balsa!" he exclaimed as if to make it

clear that he was more than familiar with the story. "So *magnifico* it has changed my life," he went on, stirring his creamy white brew. "It happened at just the right time for me, just the right time," he mused, repeating this more to himself than to me.

His name was Alvin Kinear, and he had come from Colorado. Back in college at Lawrence, Kansas, he had been active in student politics for the year and a half of his campus stay. Then he got the urge to travel, to see the world and "find himself." That was two years ago. His Marco Polo route had taken him to India and a guru, to Ceylon and a Buddhist teacher, to New Guinea and Australia for a friendly brush with the aborigines.

Four months ago he had landed in Sydney and found a "cool pad" in King's Cross hippieland, where he had been living with no plans or directions for the days ahead. Money was apparently no object. He traveled lightly and cheaply and was not averse to working at odd jobs along the way. Now, after his vagabonding and a bout with drugs and grass, everything had suddenly melted into futility. Gurus and Zen, the lure of the aboriginal "dreamtiming," rap sessions at counter-revolution meetings—things he used to enjoy—had of late become meaningless and full of frustration. Recently he had felt a terrible conformity in the vaunted non-conformist style of the liberalized generation of which he was a part. Their symbols of peace had begun to haunt him with their sense of neutralism about everything. The way of the world, a place *in* the world, money, morals, all had become annoyingly irrelevant.

Into this sense of hopelessness came the sunburst of *La Balsa*. To Alvin, the adventure instantly became a legend and a symbol, catching his imagination and focusing him on the thought that every person is an explorer in his own right by the very nature of existence. Every life, he concluded, is a raft by virtue of the fact that we are all confronted by the ocean of time.

He put his idea about the rightness of the world into simple terms: "It is up to every individual to decide how he is going to handle the raft."

Sweeping aside questions which might have challenged the general assumption that some individuals seem destined to have smoother sailing and better rafts —yachts, for example—he pursued his point:

"The raft is the thing. That's where we're tested and that's where what we really are shows up. A man should prove something, you know? The *La Balsa* crew proved this thing about Indians making the trip. Okay. We've all got to prove something. That's been my trouble. I wasn't proving anything, only that I wanted to escape. I was running and drifting."

It so happened that I knew what he meant because of a memory out of the years when I was his age. My geographical runaway may not have matched his, except as far as futility and frustration were concerned. But the world had seemed lacking in rightness in my student days, too, and had there been a drop-out trend I would have joined the movement. There were generation gaps and credibility gaps then, as now.

But one day on our campus a speaker came to lecture about a raft on which he had spent twenty-one days without food or water. He talked about his feelings and his fears and that night, I recalled, I could not sleep because he had awakened in me an awareness similar to Alvin's: life is a raft, time is the sea, and the rightness about the world is that it forces everyone to prove his intrinsic worth.

The lecturer had been James Whittaker. The epic he talked about was the time he and Captain Eddie Rickenbacker crash-landed in the Pacific, that loneliest of oceans. That experience in 1942 also pushed the customary news from the papers of the globe. When I heard Whittaker tell his story I lived through every harrowing moment with him. I felt the breath of hope in every prayer he prayed. I saw the face of God veiled in the hours of despair and saw Him smiling in the miracle moments of certain faith. There were times when I, too, thought I heard the angels sing.

I was there when the sea swallow landed on Rickenbacker's head: food sent from God out of nowhere. I believed Whittaker when he related how a black cloud mysteriously appeared and provided water when they were dying of thirst. I could understand the contracts he made with God if only he would be saved. All were responses I had felt in some degree on my own raft of life, and the world became more "right" when I realized that we can never touch the deeper reaches of our nature unless something challenges and tests our greatness along the way.

I was sure that my raft would never be the same after that, especially since it was my privilege to escort Whittaker around the campus during his stay. His courage and perspective on life rubbed off on me, and though I forgot him through the years, the nearness of the encounter was apparent when I thought of it in the light of *La Balsa* the magnificent!

Life is the raft; or, better, the raft is life. The *cappucino* game Alvin and I played as we talked about these analogies resulted in scribbled notes on the margins of the newspaper, homespun graffiti that said:

The Raft

1. Your raft is as strong as you build it.

2. Its construction involves ingenuity, selection of materials, knowledge of construction.

3. Take advantage of the wisdom of earlier raftsmen. After all, the builders of *La Balsa* were inspired and guided by the exploits of Thor Heyerdahl and his immortal *Kon-Tiki*.

4. Your raft's reliability must match the challenge of the sea. Determine the area of life's adventure and plan accordingly. The greater the challenge, the sturdier must be your raft. What do you want to conquer, a millpond or the Pacific?

5. Recognize that there may be times when you will be thrown overboard. That is no disgrace, especially during a storm.

6. Beware of sharks.

7. Recognize that the journey consists of days of calm as well as days of turbulence.

8. Become knowledgeable in the matter of natural currents, winds, and the rules of navigation. In other words, "Catch the drift of things."

9. Rely upon your innate gifts and resources, but when these have been exhausted, expect a miracle.

10. Choose your raft partners with care and consider the need for an affinity of spirit among the crew.

11. Assume a full measure of personal responsibility. If you embark on an adventure, be adventurous.

12. Live with the universe as though it were friendly.

13. Keep your eye on the goal and on what you are trying to prove.

14. Stay on course.

15. Do not despair if somewhere along the way your raft scrapes a reef and needs a tow. This may prove to be a lesson in humility or in the art of intercommunication.

16. Have faith that the end of the journey justifies the trip and that the final goal is but another beginning.

Minette the cat? In our analysis she became the symbol of affection and of the pleasure we derive from things we possess as well as from those which attach themselves to us. They are ours for a while. We are their custodians, but we know we must eventually let them go. Their spirit may persist with us unendingly, but they, too, have their own rafts to ride and their own lives to live.

Poor Minette. She was not allowed to set her paws on Australian soil due to quarantine regulations. She would have to spend the rest of her life at sea and was already being adopted by a lonely freighter crew. Minette, the law decreed, was a cat without a country.

The law. Sometimes the law is more a matter of order than of mercy, more concerned with the letter than with the spirit of things. But then, Minette was lucky. And the freighter crew was lucky, and sometimes when man's law means it for evil, a higher law means it for good.

After all, Minette had her moment, as everyone has sometime in life. Her big moment came when each member of the *La Balsa* crew fondled her for the last time, stroked her black fur tenderly and whispered how he loved her, telling her what a rare, good sport she had been to make the long and perilous journey without so much as a disgruntled meow.

"By-by, Minette. God bless you. Just having known you tells me there is someting right with the world."

She heard the words in four different languages and they were all the same to her. Then she was passed into the outstretched hands of the rugged freighter crew who held her tenderly.

"By-by, Minette."

As for Alvin, he had his own ideas as to which way his raft would be heading. "I'm anxious to go home," he said.

"Even if it is against the current?" I joked.

"Even so," he agreed. "Just now it all seems very much on course."

So we shook hands and parted. He went his way and I went mine.

A feeling of rightness and a sense of deep meaning came over me. After all, the four adventurers on the "chip of a raft"—and Whittaker on his, Alvin on his, I on mine, and the millions who made up our current passenger list—weren't we all in the same boat, so to say? Wasn't it wonderful to know that there would still be challenges and mysteries ahead for each of us as we sailed the sea of time?

As I folded up the story, something within me said, *"Viva La Balsa, magnifico!"*

.7.

The Kennel

He was obviously a mongrel, a cross between a sheepdog and a spitz, but the matter of his breed was incidental. He was healthy and proud and alive with life, all thirty-two pounds of him, a happy, openhearted dog if ever I saw one. Although filled with exuberance he heeled as if obediently on leash—which he wasn't—and as trusting of his master as his master was of him.

I was checking in at New York's East Side air terminal when they entered. The snappy step of the stocky middle-aged man jauntily wearing a black beret caught my attention. But the dog, walking briskly at his owner's side, took my eye. His coat was shaggy gray with patches of brown. A brown ring of hair circled his left eye like a kooky monocle of some new life style. White tail wagging, he greeted the sparsely peopled mid-morning terminal with an attitude that said all's right with the world.

His name was Celsus. I heard it loud and clear when in a mixture of German and French his master explained that he wanted tickets to Denver not only for himself but also for Celsus.

"Celsus!" he repeated, pointing to the happily obedient bundle of fur standing knee-high at his side.

The serious-faced ticket agent behind the counter

leaned over to apprise the situation. Celsus raised his eyes to return the compliment, stuck out a healthy red tongue and wagged his tail.

"Setz dich!" whispered his master, and then, to prove that the dog was bilingual, added, *"Asseyez-vous!"*

Celsus instantly sat down.

"You can't take the dog with you on the plane," the agent explained. "He must be put in a shipping kennel."

The bereted client's expression made it clear that his understanding of English was limited. Looking around hopefully for help, he caught my eye. I decided that if he stuck to German I might be of help.

"Do I understand correctly," he accosted me in strong Teutonic terms, "that my Celsus cannot ride with me even if I buy him a ticket? He stands nineteen inches. I can hold him in my lap. He must go in a box? Not Celsus. He is more human than some people. Since I came to this country three months ago he has been my best friend. I found him when he was lost and I trained him. You think he makes trouble? Look at him!"

I *was* looking at his lovable off-breed companion, and I decided then and there that if I owned the airline I would instantly rewrite the regulations. Celsus was not only a gentleman who wouldn't smoke or pace the airplane aisles, he was discipline personified. When he heard *"Setz, dich,"* he sat as if proud to show his quick response to every whispered command.

It was no use, however. Rules are rules, and with some ticket agents dogs are dogs. Celsus was doomed for a box if he wished to fly.

A look of agony swept his master's face when a young, personable airline assistant suddenly appeared bearing a cardboard kennel. This canine container shocked me, too. It was in the shape of a truncated, six-sided pyramid, with six top flaps that ingeniously overlapped, and air holes perforated in the sides. The "kennel man" also brought a rope for tying around the box once Celsus got inside.

The most distressing feature about it all was that the kennel seemed somewhat smaller than the dog. This caused my friend in the beret to wince, as if he himself were to be placed inside. We had a heated discussion about the dimensions, but the ticket agent's patience was running out, especially since the line of passengers was lengthening and the airport limousines would soon be rolling in.

To think of Celsus riding all the way to Denver among bags and baggage was bad enough. It was plain torture to think of him in a box in which he could hardly stand upright.

But one by one the legal steps in the inevitable foreclosure of the rules were effected. The six flaps were opened by the kennel man while the sheepdog watched with infinite interest. He knew what it was all about, you could bet on that. Somewhere during the six or seven years of his canine existence he had learned to look with patient wonder on the world, and he looked on in wonder now. Tongue out, he cocked his monocle-circled eye in a knowing glance at his master as if to say, "We've gone through worse things than this together, you and I."

Hans Scheib was not so sure. He had given me his name as if hopeful that this would warrant a somewhat better break than he or Celsus had gotten up to now. But even his Swiss status did not help. There stood the open box, waiting like a trap for its casually submissive victim. His master could have said, *"Hupf!"*and the dog would have jumped into the kennel. But instead, Hans swallowed hard and gathered Celsus gently in his arms with a flow of loving German endearments. As he embraced his pet and deposited him inside that cardboard hexagon, you'd have thought he was placing a living sacrifice on the altar of the unknown God.

"You must bend down a bit, my good boy," Hans whispered in German. "The box is all they have, and there is no time to find a bigger one. So, you bend down. Good. Very good."

It was almost too easily done. The kennel man, closing the sturdy flaps one by one, was noticeably pleased at the expeditious way it was all working out, and the ticket agent paused in his transactions with a passenger to give the job an approving glance. His self-satisfied demeanor said better than words, "You see, ladies and gentlemen, if you will just listen to us and not argue with us, everything moves smoothly and in order. We know what we are doing or we wouldn't be in this business. You see how efficiently this operation was executed?"

But when he resumed his work, we saw what he did not see. We saw a moist, black nose poke its way through a crack in the flaps and then a white fuzzy tail emerged through another crack as happily as if it were a banner of victory proudly waving. It was quite a sight, and several of the onlookers who had been watching the operation applauded loudly and gathered round.

"*Ach,* Celsus!" exclaimed Hans Scheib in a voice of half joyous wonder and half despair.

"Wait a *minute!*" said the kennel man. "You've got plenty of air in there to breathe! Down, boy, down!"

With this he proceeded to push the dog's snoot and tail back out of sight.

Hans protested in no uncertain Germanic terms. "You don't shove my dog's nose down!" he ordered. "Open that kennel box and do things decent, you hear? If the box must be bigger, we get a bigger one. You don't push my Celsus around, understand?"

The young man understood the spirit if not the language of the orders and hastily opened all six flaps. At this, of course, Celsus stood up proud and erect, stuck out his tongue and waggled his brush-like tail as if to ask his master how he was doing.

"Ach, mein Junge!" Hans lamented. That brief utterance betrayed both pride and agony in what was going on. "You see, Celsus," he explained as he knelt down and gently stroked his lovable pet, "there are times we must go through things like this. You must lie down like a good boy. Lie down even if it is cramped. You understand?"

Of course Celsus understood. He instantly squatted down and cocked an eye to assure his master that he had his wits about him. As for the reminder that there are things one must go through in life even if one feels cramped, that was part of the game which Celsus apparently knew instinctively.

As the kennel man applied himself to a businesslike resumption of closing the flaps, I could not help thinking of a friend of mine, a common everyday jack-of-all-trades man-about-town, who lived with the same rhythmic ease and acceptance of life that Celsus was displaying. I had often envied him because of the way he took life in stride. He never seemed to fight against circumstances, and yet he had them in control. He bowed to the inevitable as Celsus bowed to the kennel, but I always had the feeling that he was in control, as Celsus seemed to be.

The thought was electrifying, for in a flash I sensed a rightness about the world which comes not from without but from *within*. A dog or a man standing in command of himself, of his inner self—poised, confident under all circumstances—projects upon life a secret of the ages: *that which I am is stronger than that which is imposed upon me!*

For a transfigured moment I was no longer in an air terminal. I was with my jack-of-all-trades finding joy and meaning in life. I was being led through history, in and out of the lives of people who had caught the ebb and flow of the universe as it played upon them with all its stresses and strains and made them realize their inner resources. From a Dostoevski who "found God" in a prison camp to a Messiah who "proved God" in the harmony of his life, I saw myself in situations where *I* had wondered how in heaven's name it would all come out. Now I laughed to myself to think how powerful the force of an attitude can be and how wondrous the impact of a philosophy actually is when demonstrated in dog or man!

I had never realized the depth of this truth until just now. Think of the books on self-improvement and self-reliance I had read! Think of the courses in religion and philosophy I had taken! Think of the sermons I had listened to and the wise sayings I had memorized and the beliefs I had so confidently professed! Yet, when it came to the pinch of life there had usually been something wanting, and when it came to finding a rightness about the world, there had always been too much mystery about it for comfort.

Now with a vision of Celsus and his sturdy acceptance of the inevitable, I too was growing in understanding and in faith.

How did Celsus get to be this way, and where had my jack-of-all-trades found his secrets and truths to live by? Evidently there are moments of revelation which some earthlings are wise enough to catch and use for self-fulfillment while others pass them by. There must be a matrix or matrices that play on life, and if we are wise enough and insightful enough we learn that they are sent to mold us into something higher than the ordinary level of being.

The history of dogs had always fascinated me because of its parallels in the history of man. At some point the partnership between dog and man was consummated in trust and awareness, even as man's relationship with God was sealed in understanding somewhere along the way. The breakthrough moment came when the dog trusted man and man trusted the dog. The moment of spiritual progress dawned when man trusted God, and God, man.

So thinking, it was no longer a case of "Poor Celsus!" As far as I was concerned, it was, "Mighty Celsus!" *Para-Celsus,* if you like, for this mongrel had the situation in perfect control, even though the determined kennel keeper had him once more securely in the box and even though his solicitous master was reassuring him that this was the way life had to be at times and that there was no way out of the inevitable. After all, when you came right down to it, Celsus was going on a trip and embarking on a great adventure, even though it may not have been first class.

Isn't every day of life a trip of some sort for all of us, mongrels or pedigreed, whatever we may be?

Celsus had the truth built into him. His tail kept wagging and his eyes were smiling down to the closing flip of the sixth and final flap. The sweet and trusting dog was now fully inside, tail, snoot, brown-circled eye and all. There wasn't a whine or a whimper out of him. Mighty Celsus in harmony with his world!

I was happy to see the problem resolved because my limousine was being announced and I had already over-stayed my time. Still I waited long enough to see the kennel man wrap the rope around the box. Deftly he wound the sturdy strands in an intricate criss-cross pattern. Then he proceeded to make a masterly loop at the top, a convenient handle by which the cargo could be carried now that the job was done.

I gave the scene a lingering glance: Hans Scheib touched his beret reverently in something like a fond salute. The check-in people smiling understandingly, the ticket agent officiously going about his duties, the increasingly busy terminal, the concealed and silent Celsus, all were photographed in my mind.

Now the kennel keeper's strong hand grasped the loop on the sheepdog's box preparatory to carrying it away. As he did so a most unprecedented thing happened. He lifted the kennel all right, but by some inexplicable trick of fate, the bottom suddenly burst open. The box and the rope dangled limp in his hands, and Celsus stood free and upright on the terminal floor, tail waggling, tongue out, moist eyes beaming up at his master, head pleasantly cocked at all who cared to see.

"Gott in Himmel!" cried Hans Scheib, clapping a hand to his beret. *"Miraculeux!"*

I had to agree. A miracle to be sure! This Houdini-like escape was also a final reminder that nothing can ever conquer a soul in harmony with itself! Then and there I told myself that we simply *must* learn that beyond the reach of our capabilities is a love and power infinitely greater than our own. Just now, for a moment at least, the rightness of the world was found in the divine imagining that God really and truly watches over life!

Before hurrying to my limo, the last words I heard were those of the young kennel man assuring Hans that a larger and sturdier box would be forthcoming. He would find one, rest assured. If not, he would make doubly certain this one would be reinforced.

Either way, it mattered little to Celsus. He was where he was, ever in the right place at the right time.

During my ride to the airport, I already saw him in my mind's eye at the end of his journy, standing confident and serene as if to say, "Well, we all have our kennels now and then."

With him stood those human beings I knew who, like my jack-of-all-trades, looked on life mildly and with patient faith as if there were always something beyond, above, within the whirling world that spoke of simple things, and held a generous measure of love and trust and winsome joy in every circumstance.

One doesn't catch this rightness about the world unless he sees it with an inner eye—or, better, first sees himself in full command, no matter how cramped or dark the flight.

.8.

The 747

Recently I flew home from a global trip on the 747. This biggest of the strato-cruisers takes off and comes down as gallantly as a seagull, effortlessly carrying its 400 passengers through oceans of space at 625 miles an hour.

Concealed in its intricate and fascinating anatomy are forty miles of wire circuitry, mazes of technical devices, networks of electronic arteries and nerves, capillaries of gears and gadgets—4,500,000 separate parts to be exact, all functioning flawlessly, all synchronized in the wonder of man's creative skill and targeted to the common cause of getting its occupants safely to where they want to go, in record time.

Despite the question of planes polluting the atmosphere and other challenges, admiration for the astro-liner was fresh in my mind when I disembarked at the Los Angeles airport. Here I was met by my friend Jay who took the joy out of my enthusiasm by his greeting.

"Things are in a holy mess all around the world, aren't they?" he complained.

"Somebody told me that in Southeast Asia," I assured him testily.

Somebody had—not only in Asia, but in the subcontinent and in the Middle East and elsewhere along the way. But I realized again that you need not travel to far-off places to get the message. Your best friend will tell you.

I took a backward look at the 747. There it stood, a proud bird in a colony of smaller doves of various colors and sizes. Poised and alert, it seemed already eager for the signal to take off again. If man can make transports as fabulous as these, I told myself, there must be *something* right with his world. In fact, evidence of creative rightness was all around us as we walked through the teeming terminal, down the escalator, through the mural-decorated corridor and onto the moving walkway. We picked up my bags at the shining carousel and strode out through doors that opened automatically when they saw us coming.

Jay's sports car was waiting in the bright sunlight. He turned on the radio. Not satisfied with the program, he switched to a built-in cassette, and instantly the L.A. symphony did a command performance.

We drove to his home overlooking the city and the ocean and the surf and the sailboats and the yachts, and there was music piped into every room in his Monterey-type house, even out onto the patio where we relaxed. Jay's attractive wife Kay, lovely in a red housecoat, joined us with refreshments, and as we sat in the sunshine wonder of it all, in the midst of camellias in bloom and lush and lovely bougainvillea all over the place, Jay soliloquized, "Man, this old world, what's it coming to!"

His wife intervened, "Oh, now, just a minute, darling!" She spoke lightly, but still the feeling persisted that the world "out there," the big world, *was*, by common acclaim, in a mess. Apparently that world, the macrocosm, so impinged upon the personal world, the microcosm, that it bedeviled it with doubt.

Then something happened. Jay's nine-year-old son Nickie sauntered to the patio to show off the portable TV his dad had given him for his birthday. There were three colored sets in the house, but Nickie had to have one he could carry around when he wasn't using his cassette recorder or riding his cantilever bike.

So the boy paraded in front of us, his enchanted audience, with the mini-TV perched on his head.

The program flickering on the 6 by 9 inch screen happened to be a news review which, at the moment, showed the release of diplomat John Cross, who had been held hostage for sixty days by the Quebec Liberation Front. Cross described how he had been held in a sunless room throughout his ordeal, how he had been constantly threatened by his abductors, how they kept him within killing range, and how on occasion they strapped sticks of dynamite to his head to intimidate him.

Cross was saying, "The greatest thing I learned about my world is that I never realized or appreciated the wonder and the value of the ordinary, everyday things in life, the things we usually take for granted."

Then there was a scene of Mrs. Cross as she welcomed her husband into her arms, and we caught the drama of the reunion as Nickie marched back into the house, the TV still adroitly balanced on his head.

This interlude of Nickie and the TV was like something out of a Greek drama, a *deus ex machina* magically appearing out of nowhere and returning to nothingness, but leaving an unforgettable impression. Kay leaned back in her chaise longue and closed her eyes.

"I once heard," she said as though she were suddenly far away, "if you want to appreciate anything, just imagine that everything you have is suddenly lost, and then imagine you get it all back."

There was a period of silence, then "That's right, Kay," Jay agreed in a quietly changed voice.

We sat saying nothing. The total impact of world conditions was still real. I could still hear people around the world complaining that things are in a mess, as Jay had said, but just now we sat in a *new* world. Just now we recognized an inner awareness which told us that before we can think clearly about global affairs, we must be able to think clearly about ourselves. Before we can appreciate what is most needed in the world we must appreciate what we have. We cannot project a new consciousness into the environment until we have developed a new consciousness within.

Though continually urged to cope with the world from a bargaining basis of reality, of power and strength, just now I was thinking what might conceivably happen if someone started meeting the world from a basis of thankfulness and love.

Something was *right* with the world, and just now that rightness was beyond words. It was a feeling.

I thought of the good earth, nature's world, as I had seen it from the air during the weeks of my flight. I remembered the hurrying scenes I had seen from the ground, the people's world, in which the work and worship of the masses made all worlds one. There was no easy answer to the questions of war, hunger, disease, suffering and man's exploitative inhumanity to man. But there had been scarcely a moment during my trip when I did not say to myself that if man can make the kind of plane he wants to fly in, he can surely make the kind of world he wants to live in.

Who, on returning from a flight, has not thought

about the wonder of man's technological world? A few hours ago I had been in Japan and now I was here. How marvelously exciting the whirling earth actually was! How a person would like to take the people of all nations into his arms and share his longing and his sense of wonder with them!

But as I was sentimentally thinking along these lines, Jay came abruptly out of his own momentary fantasy with a question. Turning to his wife he recalled, "That thing you said, Kay, about losing everything and getting it back. That sounds good. But what if a person loses everything and doesn't get it back?"

"I know," she nodded understandingly. "I know what you mean."

I now remembered that before I went on my trip, there had been rumors about Jay's financial setbacks and the round of difficulties he was having with his industrial projects.

"Get what I mean?" Jay asked me pointedly. "What if a man *doesn't* get it back?"

"Then," I had to say, "I suppose we must take an inventory and see what resources we have left."

"And if there aren't any left?"

"That brings us back to the 747," I found myself saying, but instantly realized this was rank tactlessness since Jay's dilemma was directly tied in with a thoroughly depressed aerospace industry. Thousands of aerospace personnel were out of work on the West Coast. Jay's projects had been caught in the midst of this cycle.

"The 747," he reflected warily, and shook his head.

Since I had gone this far there was little I could lose by at least explaining what was on my mind. I tried to say that the strato-cruiser with its miles of wiring, its electronic wonders, its gears and gadgets, its multi-million parts, is really a mirror of man himself. Man made it, made it out of ideas and dreams, out of mental magic and the skill of technological thought; made it cooperatively, synchronizing its myriad details until he had it in the air, a living thing.

My point was that whoever and whatever made *us* created such a phenomenal combination of parts and pieces that up until now no one has been able to make an accurate count of the anatomical bits which that Master Craftsman fitted together. I was thinking of the inexplicable wonder of man as an individual. The greatness of man, the marvel of an individual, stripped of everything he owns or has or holds. That was the analogy I was awkwardly trying to explain. The simple fact of *being*. Mind, body, soul, thought, passion, love—life's 747.

Was it possible that as our continual talk about the wrongness of the world had ruled out any rightness, so the seeming misery of the macrocosm had blinded us to the beauty and potential of the microcosm Self? Had the trappings of life, our false values, our rush after phenomenal *things* also made us unaware of the greatness of our multi-phased capacity for rising above material losses and beginning all over again?

Analogies are never perfect, to be sure, and to compare a strato-cruiser to a person of flesh and blood might be unallowable. Still, Jay and Kay were sufficiently good hosts to let me go on with my surmising. An individual, I insisted, is no less an individual because he has been stripped of his resources, any more than the 747 was less powerful simply because it stood docked at the air terminal devoid of passengers and cargo. It still had its same dynamic essentials and capabilities. The central inner force common to all substantial crafts, and yet a force unique in each, was still intact. All it needed was to be readied again for flight.

"That," Jay mused, going along with the analogy, "requires a crew. It requires people who believe in you. People you can trust and who trust you."

"And a co-pilot," Kay spoke up. "I'm right here."

Jay was visibly affected. "There couldn't be a better one," he told her.

"I was thinking even more," I said, "about the comparison psychologically. History is full of accounts of people who discovered power and resources within themselves, not only after they lost material things and started over again, but even after they had become handicapped—or left for dead, for that matter. There are resources within us in the way of ideas, will, determination, creativity which by the very nature of things seem to be released under stress."

We conceded that in each life it is our consciousness of the rightness of the world *within* that causes us to rise above ourselves. It is the awareness of our divine functioning that gets us started again, gets us off the ground.

Kay leaned back in her chair. With a light laugh she suggested that now for the first time she realized why she had taken a year of pre-med training. Her physician father had once encouraged her to follow his profession, but it was not for her. Nonetheless, since we had piloted the 747 straight into the subject at hand, she was quite prepared to help us out. It was surely true, she agreed, that just as an airplane has resource back-up functions equipping it not only for normal flying but for emergencies as well, so is man similarly equipped. The analogy was not as farfetched as it first appeared.

In make-believe professorial fashion she recalled some academic indoctrination. "The physical body," she expounded, "is so constructed that its preservation is aided by prompt response to danger and instant adaptation to environmental change. When the individual is threatened or attacked, life's chain reactions are triggered, preparing the individual to either fight or flee. The heart beats more forcefully, breathing becomes deeper, more sugar is pumped into the blood, the sense organs alert the nervous system and arouse to action the endocrine glands. Even pain sets off its warning alarm and has its constructive function, and the intricate mechanisms of the brain marshall hitherto seemingly unknown forces to the rescue. Is that what you mean by life's 747?"

She probed her memory further to recall how the muscles of the body, six hundred and fifty-six of them, cooperate to generate motive power; how the countless millions of cells are arranged to work together unerringly; how the billions of nerve fibres are mysteriously interrelated and controlled by a central computerized system; how the trillions of blood cells, the thousands of platelets, the circulatory system, the heart, spinal column, bones, tissues, the whole incredible inner world unites to become a creative cosmic center, starting from scratch to build man's outer world in the same way that God originally created man from the "dust of the earth."

"I do believe, Jay," Kay said, "there is something to be said for all we're saying." "I've never questioned it," Jay agreed defensively. "I know we have inner resources. I know the mind is geared to new ideas. I've always bet everything I've ever done on that."

"Then," said Kay, "all we have to do now is bet

everything on it again. You see, darling, creatively you have more now than when you started out originally. Right?"

Jay agreed. I could sense what was going through his mind. I could see his deepened appreciation of Kay. I could feel his growing realization of all he had to be grateful for, how his hope was being restored again and how the world at large was righting itself because of the rebirth of his world within.

Some moments are beyond words, and these moments were some of them. Something higher and greater than ourselves must surely have a part in situations of this kind. If there was any doubt about it, it was soon dispelled, for out of the house came Nickie as if borne once again by the *deus ex machina,* an innocent player in the drama, carrying in his hands a small, fragile model plane. Absorbed in it, a look of concern on his face, he walked to where Jay sat in thought.

"Look at this dumb thing, Dad," he said, "the aileron is all fouled up again. *You* can fix it."

Jay took the plane and held it up against the sky to examine it. "If I can't fix it," he reflected, "your mother can."

"There's nothing your daddy can't fix," Kay told him. "Remember that."

I thought just then that though I had heard it said in many parts of the globe that things are in a mess, I had also experienced, in homes and cultures along the way of my trip, moments of wonder and love fully as meaningful as these.

There must be something right with a world like this.

.9.

The Carousel

He said, "I'll tell you what's right
with the world: *friends*. Friends who love you and accept
you for what you are, regardless of what you may happen to be. True, some people insist that the best of
friends are those who pinpoint your faults so that you
may correct them, who psychoanalyze your weaknesses
so that you may overcome them, who remind you of
your potentials so that you can improve them. But give
me the friend who takes you for better or worse and
who has the insight to know that if he loves you without
wanting to remake you, you will be smart enough to
catch on to the greater good still half-asleep within
yourself.

"I'll tell you something else that's right with the
world: *taxi drivers*. Taxi drivers who treat you as if you
were favoring them by getting into their cab instead of
resenting the fact that you waved them down. It stands
to reason that it's no easy job to buck the traffic on a
ten-hour day and to keep your temper in crowded, busy
streets, especially when your last fare was probably a
schmoe. But the art of cabbie-kindness is one of the
most important factors of metropolitan life; it has
created or broken many a man's respect for the
megalopolis in which he first felt the mood and heartbeat of the inner city.

"Or take *waitresses*. There's another thing that's right, waitresses who have the magic touch, who can sense how others feel. Few public servants catch us in more extreme or changeable moods. Think for a minute what you're like when you go into a restaurant. You are hungry and tired, or maybe not hungry and full of life. You are alone and depressed or with a crowd and feeling gay. You look at the prices. They are too high and you get defensive, or they're too low and you get suspicious. The menu is too involved or too simple. You are in a hurry or you don't want to be hurried. You want attention but you don't want to be over-attended. Along comes a waitress with the magic touch. She catches and understands your mood, whatever it is. I've often wondered if she knows how important she is in the merry-go-round of life.

"Want to know what's right with the world? *The Guide Dog.* Talk about a man giving his life for a friend, what about an animal giving his life for a man? When I see a Seeing-Eye dog taking a man through city streets, I get to thinking something pretty basic, about how way back in the beginning of life the first dog and the first man must have met somewhere in the jungle and felt a companionship deep and sincere, deeper than most relationships we know. There must have been a time when the very fact of survival formed a bond that linked all living things. We've sort of lost that, but maybe there will come such a time again. What do they call it? Kinship of all life? I see it moving like a vision through the crowded traffic whenever the Guide Dog and his companion pass that way. A sightless man once told me that the leash connecting him to his dog was love, and that it ran both ways.

"What's right with the world? *Champions.* Champions in any field. They make me stop and think about their dedication, their discipline, their determination, all of which they hide from you and make whatever they are doing seem easy. They've caught a rhythm. The rhythm of something we don't usually see and which we feel only at odd times. Sure, some people are born with special talent. There has always been the mystery of how geniuses and prodigies come to be. Sometimes that doesn't seem fair. But as far as I'm concerned, any overview of a champion—the best acrobat, the best ballerina, the best skier, golfer, juggler, tight-rope walker, chess expert, home run king; the greatest jockey, swimmer, diver, stuntman, tennis star or Ping-pong artist —tells me that somewhere in this life or in a previous time around he earned the right to be crowned the champion *this* time around. I don't have any greater admiration for anyone, unless it's the runner-up who has worked as hard but loses, and then comes up and congratulates the winner. Champ or near-champ, at such a time, proves there is something right with the world.

"Or take moments."

"Moments?" I asked.

"*Moments*. There are moments that tell me there's something right with the world. Moments when Whatever and Whoever is out there is also in here, in me. Moments when there is nothing to fear, nothing to figure out, nothing to be looked for, nothing to be envied, nothing to be desired. Nothing, but just to *be*. I have never had it explained how these moments come or why or when, and I don't know that I want to. I only know that they happen, and something tells me that as long as I live, no matter what happens otherwise, there will always by these moments. Maybe you send them to me or I to you. Who knows?

"I feel the same way about letters," he went on to say.

"*Letters* can be something that's right with the world. Mail plays a more important part in the daily carousel than we care to admit. I mean personal mail of the kind a friend of mine has in mind when he says to the post-master in the little town where he lives, 'Is there anything for me today that will change my life?'

"He has his own inner security, but his question is more than a phrase. Get a letter from someone who wants nothing more than to be remembered and to remember you, from someone who has something encouraging, flattering, lighthearted or profound to say, and you settle back more comfortably in your niche in life. Often when I reread letters of this kind, I slip a piece of stationery in the typewriter and send a note to someone who needs to find this kind of rightness in his mailbox, too.

"What else is right is *nature.* We are suddenly taking an ecological approach to it and that is understandable in view of what we have done to it, but sometimes we forget that nature is nearer and more compressed than we realize.

"We want expansive views and quiet spots and countryside, all of which are good things. We want hills, lakes, forests. But nature's wonders can be found in a blade of grass or in a single flower or in a pair of robins grubbing for worms to feed their young. This is where the inspiration for ecological understanding begins. It begins not in the law, but in the love of things.

"To appreciate the wonder of nature, a person need not see an ocean. He can find it in a raindrop. He needn't live in the forest. A city park or even a solitary tree can give him food for thought. A cocoon in my little garden told me more about life and death than came to me in many a sermon.

"The city is my home. This is where I have always lived, but when I was a boy this was open country. As life would have it, I stayed here when the area became first a neighborhood, then suburbs, and now very much a part of the city. I like to feel that underneath the transformation nature still has its place of quiet around me, and that every change of season, every turn of day, counts me in its scene as long as I have the will to watch it play its game.

"Sometimes I don't fully agree. But that's another thing that's right with the world. *Quarrels.*"

"Quarrels?" I repeated with a laugh.

He laughed lightly, too. "Husband-wife quarrels," he said. "A friend-to-friend quarrel, kids' quarrels, and it may even be that in some distant day nations will discover that there is something right and helpful about quarrels they have over borders, boundaries, tariffs and the like.

"I have heard it said that in ancient times when Oriental rulers had something legitimate to quarrel about, they would meet together in an open field. There in the heart of nature their respective armies would march in and stand fully caparisoned face to face. Then the rulers would ask each other, 'Now, if our men were to engage in battle, which army do you suppose would win?' They would sincerely evaluate the situation from every conceivable angle and arrive at an answer without a shot being fired or a spear being thrown. Then they and all their men would have a cup of tea. So the dispute was settled.

"Somewhere, out of a quarrel, truth long hidden should by rights emerge. Always, out of the right kind of quarrel, a greater truth is born. The most wonderful rightness about a quarrel is that if properly conducted, it leaves the atmosphere clearer and the relationship dearer than before. This should be true even of quarrels a person has within himself.

"The comparison of a lover's quarrel to a thunderstorm is an image used many times in sentimental literature, but the comparison is so good it deserves to be overworked. Anyone who has ever lived in thunderstorm country can still feel the stimulating calm and the bracing air after the storm has passed. He can still hear the thunder echoing away across the hills, as if to say that those who get no good out of quarrels must certainly lack imagination.

"Which reminds me, as I ride the carousel, the rightness of the world is best proved by the fact that things are *not* always seemingly right. When the world is really right and we are right with the world, we should welcome its unpredictableness, its uncertainty, its surprises and its innovations.

"The more I think about this, the clearer it becomes that it is this precarious quality that keeps me on my toes and gives life meaning. If the weather were always predictable, if people were always easy to figure out, if the future were cut and dried, if life were a game with the same players and the same score, I can see where things could get depressingly dull. What's really right with the world is the *unexpected!*"

Such were his opinions. When I thanked him he walked with me out-of-doors. As I looked back, I noticed he had gone into his garden where some flowers bloomed. I could not help but marvel at him as he confidently swung himself along on his crutches, a paraplegic almost since birth some forty years ago.

.10.

The Slogan

The other day a group of twelve Hutterites dropped in at our cabin in British Columbia. This is news because these collectivistically minded utopian seekers rarely leave their communes and are not given to travel or impromptu visitation. However, this contingent, which included the rugged pastor, had been picking cherries on a nearby ranch for several days and wanted to visit with my wife and me before returning to their sheltered *Bruderhof* (community of the brethren) at Pincher Creek, Alberta.

These bearded men (whom I consider the only true hippies, if by this we mean those who wish to return to nature and be self-sustaining) and these long-skirted, polka-dot scarfed women (the original flower children) have long fascinated me by virtue of the fact that out of the 129 attempts at mutualistic experiments in North America, the Hutterites alone have achieved one hundred years of uninterrupted history.

So here we were on a sparkling day on the patio overlooking Kootenay Lake and the mountains. But for the fact that the Hutterians resist being photographed, we would have taken pictures of them showing that their homespun attire was as sombre and unadorned as that worn by the first group which migrated to South Dakota from the Ukraine in 1874.

Visiting with them again impressed me with their verve and their lust for life. This delegation, consisting of three men, three boys and six young women, had a childlike eagerness for everything that caught their eye, though they coveted none of it. All they truly wanted was to be spiritual possessors for a moment of the scenic vistas, the bubbling fountain, the dancing lake, the sound of recorded music, the purr of an outboard motor, the sight of a water-skier, the fun of fellowship, laughter and a momentary taste of non-commune living.

As the bearded pastor recounted incidents of Hutterian activities and filled me in on happenings in the commune since last we saw each other four years ago, the innocence and firm security of their way of life crept into my heart. It struck me as never before that they had found a definite rightness about their world. They were truly *in* the larger world, but not of it. They saw it from the security of their cherished 3,000 acres and watched it pass as it swirled outside the *Bruderhof.* They laughed at the world's foibles, shook their heads at its wars, smiled wisely at its political machinations, grew solemn at its rush for power and murmured over its disregard for ecological law.

Lord knows I would be the last to want to join the Hutterian system! Give up my career, my hard-earned possessions, my freedom to come and go, my love for travel? Let my beard grow and see my wife in a polka-dot scarf and a homespun, colorless ankle-length dress for years on end? Find my place in the regimented routine of these ultra-Amish religionists? Not me!

Yet, as I have said, something tugged at my heart. My wife felt the tugging, too, as we noted the childlike glances of wonder at our sense of values and the inner security of their own way, the way of the commune.

In the midst of the conversation, through the sharing of soda pop and snacks and the pleasure of fooling around with a cassette (forbidden, as are radios and TVs in Hutterian homes), a slogan came to my mind. It came out of the blue of lake and sky, words I had not thought of for a long time but which a Hutterite once told me he liked better than anything he had ever heard in "my world." I attributed the slogan to author-poet Henry Van Dyke, who had a three-pronged prescription for a happy, integrated life. "See to it that you have work to enjoy, faith to believe, and someone to love."

The words struck me with subtle force. I got to thinking how often I investigate other cultures, prowl among other religions and interview people in an effort to learn their secrets and techniques. Frequently I ask famous people, wise people, academically minded men and women, "What's right with your world?" but seldom do they get through to me or I to them on a non-verbal level. Now, for a moment, the homey Hutterites put the slogan into focus simply through the force of their presence and the uncontrived simplicity of their enthusiasm. Small wonder that investigators of life in the *Bruderhof* have often concluded that the Hutterites represent our country's best adjusted ethnic group.

But psychologists and psychoanalysts had never made it clear *why* the Hutterian Brethren are as they are or what makes them tick. Now I knew. It was the living of the slogan: "Work to enjoy, faith to believe, someone to love."

Obviously, I told myself, these three ingredients must be equally proportioned. If all you do is *work*, you may turn into a robot. If you only *believe*, you may become a bore. If you insist on nothing but *love,* you may be open to suspicion. But if work, faith and love can be properly interrelated, you are well on your way to finding a certain rightness about the world, and you certainly need not be a Hutterite to make the dream come true.

Yet during this Hutterian rendezvous I did some serious thinking and probing into their philosophy and mine. Based on my close association with these utopian experimenters, I had to admit that they made the three ingredients of the slogan graphic and compelling. Take the principle of "Work to enjoy." Work to the Hutterite is an act of worship. If we are to believe them, their enjoyment of work is actually a form of gratitude for the ability of being *able* to work, a kind of thankfulness that there is work to be done and that they are physically able to perform it.

They may still adhere a bit too much to the Biblical injunction about earning their bread by the sweat of the brow and they may hold the Calvinistic glorification of the sanctity of work to be more tenable than I think it is, but they know that work is indispensable in making life worthwhile. The toil and joy of work are to them part of the world's rightness, and they claim you cannot find a truly happy person who does not have work to enjoy. The trouble with the jobless, they insist, is not that they are out of a *job,* but out of work.

When I reminded the pastor that any modern writer of Genesis would assure us that God made the world in a four-day work-week and rested on the fifth, sixth and seventh, he responded with the exhortation that a four-day week would be the surest possible way of hurrying the world to its inevitable destruction. In the commune, it is a Christian virtue of the highest order to work six full days and then keep the Sabbath holy, even to the extreme of not so much as sewing a hook-and-eye on one of their buttonless jackets.

Work to enjoy! By some divine direction and the wisdom of the elders each Hutterian boy or girl finds a niche in the workaday life of the community. If a youngster enjoys working with cattle, he will very likely someday be cattle boss. If a woman enjoys cooking, she is well on the way to becoming kitchen boss. If a girl has a fondness for geese or ducks, she can rest assured she will be the goose or duck boss, and if a young man shows an inclination for study and learning, he can get to be the teacher or the pastor of the brotherhood. In the insular world of Hutterian life—the more than 150 communes average some 100 members in each—lies a challenge for the world at large: "See to it that you have work to enjoy!"

Why shouldn't it work even better for us in our kind of world than it does for them? Our "commune" is not bound by fences nor restricted to the over-rule of elders. Our world is as large as our reach of mind and as wide and great as our ambition and creativity care to make it.

Still, the industrious Hutterite alerted me to a basic relationship of rightness that must be met in the world of every man: Work to enjoy. "We never have any labor-management problems in our world!" is the Hutterite boast. "Why should we? We are all bosses!"

They are also dyed-in-the-wool positivists when it comes to exercising the slogan's second affirmation: "Faith to believe." I sensed as never before that it is this conviction that keeps these indomitable colonists in harmony with their regimented system. Every phase of their conduct is built on the conviction that faith to believe is literally the bread of life.

I confessed to the visting pastor that some five years

ago, I had predicted that the Hutterian communes could no longer withstand the encroachments of the outside world. At that time I went on record as saying that the evening services in the communes were beginning to be neglected, the old traditions were passing, the scent of secularism was in the air. The pleasures of the American Way and the call of freedom, I insisted, were shattering the commune fences and leveling the commune gates.

Now the pastor had the laugh on me. Chortling happily at my admission, he assured me that better prophets than I had been forced to retract such impetuous prognostications. The evensongs, he testified, still close the commune day and morning prayers faithfully greet each early dawn. The loyalty of Hutterian youth is growing stronger. The devotion and dedication to commune life are on the rise. Each oncoming generation, I was told, is appreciating the merit of the *Bruderhof* more and more.

The reason? Faith to believe! Faith to believe that the Hutterian way is founded on God's decree. Had I forgotten that Acts 2:44 provides the basis for their belief? "And all that believed were together and had all things common." This, then, is faith—to believe that men of God should be different from other men and live differently than men of the secular world. Faith to believe that a brother should respect his elders, perpetuate the doctrines of his people, and recognize God's law and order in the universe. Faith to believe unquestioningly that Hutterians are on God's side and that His spirit moves in and through them in the daily run of life.

So said the pastor during our patio visit. Though I warned myself not to be carried away by his words, the fact remained that I could see and feel this "faith to believe" in the sparkling eyes and eager faces of his loyal group. There was not a shadow of doubt about their confidence in God's guidance. There was no question about their divine appointment. There was, rather, a sudden impulse to enforce their feelings with a hymn of faith.

It was really quite wonderful to hear this a cappella singing under the open sky when it is commonly heard only in the *Bruderhof.* It was reassuring to have it touch the lake and hills, especially since I had been the first, some twenty years ago, to record the hymnody of the Hutterites for the Library of Congress. Now I was reminded that these poetic expressions of faith were sung in the same nasal tone, in the same tempo and with the same depth of feeling as they have been sung for one hundred American years.

There is something thrillingly right with the world when you have the faith to believe in its rightness! Again I warned myself that I need not become a Hutterite to find this kind of spiritual orientation. All we need is the courage to live more closely to the faith that we believe. And this was equally true when it came to the last part of the slogan, which may, in fact, be first in importance.

Admittedly, nowhere in my research had I ever found such evidence that everyone in a religious fellowship had "someone to love" as I found among the Hutterites. It is love that makes their world enticing and precious. While the family unit forms the link in this Christian communal scheme, each child is loved and accepted as if he belonged to all families. He is a child of the *Bruderhof;* God's child. Psychologists who have studied and analyzed the Hutterites acknowledge that parental love and community affection give these colonists a peace and security far beyond the national norm in our society. There are no divorces among the Hutterites, and mental disorders are exceedingly rare. Crime is practically unknown, and no Hutterian has ever been in jail except for his resistance to military service.

As far as I was concerned, "someone to love" told the story of the communes as I had seen them in the Dakotas, Montana, Washington and the Canadian prairie provinces. There is abundant physical love in that way of life, and the Hutterians are the most prolific people in the world. But nowhere is sexual promiscuity more taboo and sexual perversion more unknown. In orderly fashion each marriageable member finds a mate within the chain of *Bruderhofs,* and nature keeps such a proper balance between male and female that romance rarely, if ever, reaches out beyond the commune gates.

Love is the theme and love was the topic as our group of visitors sang of God and the Hutterian way. As I listened to the singing and watched the singers sway with joy while they sang, I wondered whether they, having none of the material luxuries we enjoy—private possessions, conveniences, freedom to come and go— had therefore made a luxury out of love.

And so we visited and sang until the pastor suggested it would be good to have a prayer and then to say, *"Aufwiedersehen."* After so doing, the contingent climbed into their panel truck, their eyes bright, their attitude best expressed by one of the girls, who said, "I will live for a long time in remembrance of all that happened today." With shouts of thanks they waved farewell as the truck chugged up the winding lane and soon droned out of sight and sound.

My wife and I walked back to the patio where the

meticulous Hutterians had insisted on leaving everything immaculately clean. It was early evening and the
sun played on the lake as if reluctant to say its own
Aufwiedersehen and sink away behind the mountain's rim.
We sat for a time in the stillness while the bubbling
fountain hummed its own rhythmic song. Our schnauzer dog came up and nestled in my lap as if to scan the
freedom and the beauty of the lake and think our
thoughts.

Perhaps he felt as we did, that there are worlds upon
worlds within the great world and that every person is
actually a world within himself, and that it would be
monotonously dull if we all had the same world or the
same sense of values or even the same idea of what the
Maker of the world required of us in the way of dress
or actions or mode of life. Yet it was crystal clear that
in all these multicolored worlds and among the many
varieties of people, certain universal guidelines pointed
to universal truths. At least, just now, one such invincible directive was neatly framed into a thought-provoking slogan that said, "See to it that you have work to
enjoy, faith to believe, and someone to love."

.11.

The Singing

The sound of a Ping-Pong ball jarring the ostensibly solid doors between the Chinese mainland and America reminded me of another sound that opened a spiritual door between the U.S.S.R and the U.S.A.

It happened during a trip to Kharkov when I was traveling Intourist, Russia's official agency for accommodating visitors to the Soviet Union. Even if you can speak the language, you are in Intourist's custody, so much so that some Westerners insist it is Communism's way of keeping a watchful eye on its guests.

Viewed in another light, Intourist is also a service to facilitate and improve one's stay—a fact which my wife Lorena and I had discovered on previous visits to this largest of republic federations, a land so vast it stretches across two continents, from the North Pacific to the Baltic Sea.

Kharkov, largest rail center in the U.S.S.R., needed Intourist guides if an outsider was to catch its spirit in a ten-day stay. This city of half a million on the banks of the Udy, combining industry with culture, seemed to me committed to hard labor, but judging it through the eyes of Intourist, all was law and order and the joy of life.

Our Intourist guide was an attractive, dark-haired,

hazel-eyed girl in her mid-twenties. There was no pretense about her. Her attire was as modest as her manner. She wore makeup sparingly, had carefully manicured hands, and her open-toed shoes were better than those commonly seen in Russian stores. Most of all, she gave the impression of being a resourceful, strong-charactered person with considerable poise and capability.

Her name was Vera. She managed a small gift counter in a hotel and helped out as interpreter and guide for Intourist as needed. Assigned to us, she was sincerely interested in Lorena's plans to photograph Russian life and reservedly intrigued by my request to interview Russian religious leaders.

It was the Christmas season, and though it may have been part surmise on my part, there seemed to be something of the Advent spirit in the air. Not colored lights or crowded shops or music in the air, but nature had its date with the winter solstice here as elsewhere in the world.

One evening it snowed.

Having a vivid memory of mid-December snows which heralded my boyhood Christmases in the American midwest, I felt a keen nostaligic thrill as we walked through Kharkov streets. There *is* something special about pre-Christmas snow, especially if it falls in gentle showers on a windless night. It may be that no two flakes are ever alike, but none are different either, no matter where you roam. They touch your hands and cheeks as gently as angels' breath, and in the wintry air the flakes stay on your clothes until you get indoors, where they disappear as slyly as they came.

Falling snow and autumn leaves are memories everyone carries in his heart if he grew up where seasons change dramatically. Governments cannot rob you of the magic of it all. This phenomenon comes from a higher rightness in the world than law and order and issues from a source much deeper than politics.

Snow-wise, it was Christmas in Kharkov. The luminescent white piled up on street lamps and wires, on trees and city streets, and closed a gap between divided worlds. It also provided a world of photographic beauty through which Vera escorted my wife as our Russian adventure grew snow-decked and interesting.

Christmas, too, deserved credit for putting an appropriate focus on peace and understanding. Christmas candles burned in several homes, and occasionally an evergreen wreath could be spotted behind the flickering flame. In store windows, there were tiny cakes of wheat the legendary gift of Kolya (St. Nicholas). Dolls representing Babushka, the fabled gift-bringer, could also be seen, perpetuating the story that this adorable grandmother was still doing penance for having misdirected the Magi on their way to Bethlehem.

Being Communists, Intourist personnel are not members of a church. Vera, a dyed-in-the-wool Marxist, professed little knowledge about the state of institutionalized religion in Russia. Speculative faith, she avowed, was mostly for old people who seemed to need it. As far as freedom to worship was concerned, churches were open for Sunday services throughout the year. Protestant, Roman Catholic, Russian Orthodox, Jewish, all were available to those who needed such support, and I had visited each in turn and interviewed clerics with Vera as impartial interpreter. There was a great question in my mind as to just how tolerant the Communist control of religion was. Even though the spiritual leaders assured me they were unhampered in their work, their glances often suggested that I should form my own opinion.

They were permitted to have only Sunday services and midweek choir practice. There were no Sunday Schools or training programs and no evangelistic activity, but still it was encouraging to know that every organized governmental movement against religion had failed to stamp out a people's insistence that God should have a place in their lives. This could better be appreciated in view of the fact that at the time of the Revolution all of the churches, some 55,000, had been sealed shut. Today, fifty years later, at least 27,000 were open. When more would be permitted to function was up to the Kremlin, but realizing what a table tennis team had achieved in China, one felt that anything could happen.

One day I suggested to Vera that we would like to attend a choir rehearsal in a Kharkov church. She responded with her customary regimented courtesy and said she would make the necessary arrangements, which she did with typical dispatch. On a Wednesday evening we made our way to an Evangelical-Baptist meeting house, a white wooden structure on a side street, inconspicuously tucked away in a neighborhood of friendly homes. To reach it we had to go through a snow-packed alley where children played in the crisp dusk and where several young couples walked, apparently listening to the singing which was already in progress.

Vera seemed almost eager to share in this experience—a first for her as far as listening in on a choir rehearsal was concerned. I asked her which appealed more to her: the ornate Orthodox churches we had visited, or this plain, typically old-Protestant structure.

She replied that first she would have to be convinced of the merit of religion itself before she could judge.

"Could anyone convince you of that?" I asked.

"I don't think anyone could," she said with a laugh.

The minister who greeted us was tall, lean, middle-aged, a man unpretentious and unclerical in a brown business suit. Peering at us quizzically through the top of his bifocals, he took special note of Lorena's cameras. Picture taking was by all means permissible, he explained, but he apologized for the size of the choir. Normally it consisted of more than eighty voices, but since his people were laborers and some worked on night shifts, there were only some fifty singers in attendance this evening. They had been rehearsing for nearly an hour, not in anticipation of our coming, he assured us, but because they loved to sing.

Escorting us in under pieces of scaffolding, he announced with pride that the church was being renovated, and paused to let us look at the simple interior from beneath the balcony. The church auditorium was small, seating perhaps three hundred. It was the kind of country church one would find throughout the rural Midwest in America. On the white plastered walls were gilded Scripture texts proclaiming in Russian that "God so loved the world . . . ," "I am the Light of the World," and "Behold the Lamb of God."

The church chancel was unadorned but for a Christmas star. On the sturdy pulpit lay an open Bible. The floor was of plain boards, the pews apparently home-made. A hymn board was also reminiscent of our country churches and an upright piano with its vase of carefully arranged evergreens gave the surroundings a touch of Christmas.

The choir members, seated on a series of raised

planks against the left wall of the church, rose to their feet when we approached. Rather evenly divided between men and women, with perhaps a dozen young people in the group, they greeted us as if we were honored guests. The feeling of friendship was spontaneous and genuine. They wanted us to know we had done them a signal favor by coming. The director, a man in his early thirties, stood at a lectern, baton in hand. He insisted on introducing us to each member and proudly watched as each gave us "the right hand of fellowship."

Everyone had an enthusiastic, excited word of greeting. Some covered my hands with both of theirs and let it be known by words and expressions that Americans were welcome. "America is our Christian neighbor," they said. "Our Christian faith knows no distinction between people who believe in Him, no matter where they live."

Intourist Vera, caught in the activity of her interpreting, was apparently as thrilled as we at this royal welcome. She seemed to be saying, "You see how friendly we Russians are? This is the Motherland. These are the people and the people are the state."

The director tapped his baton on the wooden lectern. The choir sang its first number, a stirring hymn about the majesty of God. The magnificent blending of the powerful voices swept away all barriers and all differences in language or ideas. It sounded like a Cossack chorus, and during this Advent evening, as song followed song, I wished that America and Russia and all the world might have paused for just a moment to listen.

How, I wondered, could leaders fail to hear the Christmas heartbeat of their people? Where religion had this kind of self-expression, how could it fail to inspire the course of humanity? What could hold it back? Just now you wanted to say to the millions of Russians and everyone everywhere who had left the churches, "Come back and listen. One hour here, strengthened by faith, is better than your insistent attempt to prove or disprove God."

You could close your eyes and feel a spirit of universal worship. You could imagine yourself in any church anywhere in the world where people love to sing. You could make believe you were in your own home church or worshipping with people of any race or creed who shared the loneliness you felt because there is such a gulf in understanding between the rulers of the world. If only we could all get together and sing!

The over-simplification of my reverie dawned on me when at the conclusion of one of the stirring hymns, a choir member conveyed to Vera a request: "Would the visitors from America sing a song for us?"

Vera took it upon herself to intrude with an opinion of her own. She thought it an excellent idea and was sure that anyone with a name like Bach should be quite capable of filling the request, a point of view endorsed by a chorus of voices, implying that it was surely the Lord's wish that I should turn church soloist. Lorena adroitly escaped all this by suddenly becoming preoccupied with her cameras.

Not being a singer, I tried to ease out of it without offense to either the Lord or Russia by saying it was too bad no one had a violin because I would not mind playing a number—but even then I had a sinking feeling that someone might rush in with a fiddle. In fact, a dozen or more neighborly people had filtered in and seated themselves quietly beneath the balcony.

I made lame excuses about not being in voice, all of which sounded un-American. "They are not looking for musical perfection," Vera assured me, "nor do they wish to embarrass you. They just want to hear an English hymn, the kind you sing in your home church."

Suddenly I had an idea. I say "suddenly," but actually it occurred to me only after I had taken an inventory of the songs for the entire liturgical year and realized how many first lines I knew and how few verses were in my repertory. I asked Vera to inquire whether they sang *Silent Night* and, of course, they did. I suggested it would be a great idea if we all sang it together, they in Russian and I in English.

This was agreed upon with the proviso that I first sing one verse solo. This much presented no problem and I let the Christmas spirit have full sway. All I can say is that the Russian people gathered in the Evangelical-Baptist Church of Kharkov were the best (and the only) audience I ever had as a vocalist. And when I finished I was convinced that *Silent Night* is effective no matter who sings it, as long as it is sung with honest feeling during the Christmastide.

Then we sang it together. More correctly, I stood among the choir members while all around me people everywhere in Christendom were singing. The words were not Russian or English or any spoken language; they were cosmic. The event took place not in a church or in any physical location; it was enacted in celestial space.

We sang—and the shepherds watched and the "Holy Infant tender and mild" was radiantly lifted up for kings and wise men to view with insight and adoration in Bethlehem's holy manger. We sang—and surely this best-loved of all Christmas carols could not have had a more thoughtful rendition, for after the singing a hush fell over the church, a silence so deep and still that the director laid his baton on the lectern carefully with both hands lest it make a sound.

A large, husky man at my side turned to me with tears in his eyes and whispered, *"Slava Bogu,"* his words for "God be praised." The choir members turned to one another without speaking. They put their hymnals silently aside, touched their hands to their eyes and paused in solemn thought.

As I started back to the pew, they took my hand, and one by one they said, *"Mir, mir,"* which is "Peace, peace," and *"Do svidaniya"* which is "A fond farewell," and *"Spasibo"* which is more than just "Thank you." But most of all, they repeated, *"Slava Bogu."*

It was late when we walked back to the hotel with our interpreter. The alley neighborhood was very still and the white streets were deserted. Along the way a group of workmen passed us and a street car rattled by.

As we crossed an open corner, I saw the tower of an old cathedral on a hill against the moonlit sky. I had been there one day and found it abandoned, its doors boarded up. Part of the building had been converted into a factory, and I had been forbidden to enter. I wondered now whether it might have heard the Christmas voices singing in the neighborhood church, or was it much too occupied with the making of things to have time to listen?

We hardly spoke along the way back to the hotel. There was not much to say, but when we parted in the lobby and an Intourist car came to take Vera home, we said good-night and thanked her for her special attention to us and for having gone the second mile in attending to our needs.

I said to her, *"Slava Bogu*—is that better as a greeting or for saying good-by?"

She looked at us with a strangely soft and longing glance as if afraid of betraying more than she wanted us to know. "Either way," she said. "Tonight *Slava Bogu* is rather good—either way."

.12.

The Dreaming

The miracle of air travel was impressed upon me when I left Sydney, Australia, at 5:30 P.M. and arrived home in Los Angeles on the same day at *5:10* P.M. Also impressed upon me was the miraculous aspect of chance when I was told that a friend was waiting at my home, all prepared to hold me to a promise to take him to Disneyland in Anaheim the following morning. So it happened that I had the unique experience of being in down-under country one day and at Disney's magic kingdom the next, with hardly time to get the altitude out of my ears.

I realized as never before that it is a strange illusion, culturally and geographically, to measure the distance from the Australian outback to Disneyland, U.S.A., merely in terms of miles. The deception deepens when you think in terms of the relationship between the aborigines of Australia and my grown-up friend, Joel, with whom I visited the Disney wonderland. For example, you wouldn't think there is any relationship between a mountain called Uluru located in the Australian wastes of Arnhem and a man-made mountain called the Matterhorn near Anaheim, California. But on one count at least the gap closes, the distance becomes non-existent and two seemingly antithetical worlds blend into one. The unifying factor which brings these two worlds into a one-world focus is *the Dreaming.*

Obviously, Disneyland is a dream world. Everything about it is fantasy, from a submarine which submerges only two or three feet but makes you feel you are 20,000 leagues under the sea, to a realistic trip to the moon in which you are catapulted 225,000 make-believe miles without ever leaving your joggling cushioned seat. Elephants that fly, storybook characters that come to life, and even an audio-animatronic Lincoln who laughs and smiles and sheds a tear, assure you that where reality is concerned you are beyond it for the moment.

But the Dreaming I kept thinking about was more psychological than electronic. It was my interest in the Dreaming that had lured me to Australia and its aborigines. Legends about these mysterious, primitive natives had always haunted me. Their life seemed just a step removed from the jungle, and yet their extra-sensory aptitudes were sharper than ours. Though their origin was shrouded in obscurity, they had a most definite identity. In fact, when the first explorers blundered upon them in the 18th century they had no idea who these sepia-skinned people were or where they came from. Neither did the people themselves. When asked about their homeland or their migrations they simply said, "We always were."

The explorers could not comprehend a statement as simple as that. Looking only at the outward appearances, they made up their minds that these naked, freely roaming nomads were barbarians, and they began to exploit and enslave them.

Fascinating accounts of early aboriginal rites and rituals had churned in my mind during my Australian trip. I had read graphic descriptions of their initiatory and puberty ceremonies. At such times the tribal elders deliberately knocked out one or two of the upper front teeth of the boys, plucked hairs from the youngsters' heads, scarred the young bodies with sharpened jade, and gave them human blood to drink as a holy sacrament. The blood was extracted from the arms of the older men, and this oral transfusion was supposed to impart to the initiates some of the strength and wisdom of their paternal donors.

These bizarre reports, admittedly true, were only part of the story, however. What the early explorers failed to mention and what later investigators often overlooked was: the Dreaming.

The Dreaming in aboriginal culture was a time of idealistic imagining, a period of utopian longing for whatever might consistently be right with the world. In the Dreamtime, birds and beasts lived peacefully together and there was a touch of magic in the air. Man had kinship with man and all had kinship with all life.

The Dreaming was part of the initiation process. It began to unfold when the young aboriginal was escorted away from his tribe and left alone in an isolated area where he was instructed to mediate upon the ritual he had passed through. For a week or more, alone with nature, forced to fend for himself, he had time to think about his relationship with the universe. Now he reflected on the myths and legends which the elders had told him, particularly those which described how, at the beginning of the world, superhuman beings not only dreamed but *lived* their dreams. These were the hero-figures who, waking from their slumber, dared make their dreams come true. These were the giants who walked the earth, shaped the mountains, directed the rivers, carved out the valleys, caused the winds to blow and the rain to fall.

So impressive and important was this experience in

the development of youth that there is still a saying among modern Australian aborigines, "As it was in the Dreaming of old when the hero-figures were here, so let it be today."

How could I help but remember such a dreamtime period in aboriginal life as I roamed with Joel through the fairyland world that dreamer Walt Disney had created American-style? Joel, I should explain, was an aerospace engineer currently unemployed and full of discouragement. He had come down to Los Angeles from Seattle, unaware that I would just be getting back from an out-of-the-country trip. All he knew was that he had to get away for a few days, somewhere where he could think things through.

Here he was, forty-eight, scientifically trained, skilled in his profession. Yet circumstances had forced him, along with some 20,000 other aerospace specialists, out of a job. After standing in unemployment lines and worrying about keeping two children in college, he was at odds with the world. He had reached a point where he felt he could not change his vocational direction. The seriousness of the situation had obviously distressed his wife, too. She got a job as a clerk in a Seattle store and suggested he have a change of scenery and get his mind off things for a while.

"Why not," she told him one day, "go down to Los Angeles where that what's-his-name promised to take you to Disneyland."

So here we were, and what's-his-name could not help comparing life—in this case his friend Joel's life particularly—to the Dreaming. The "initiatory service," which circumstances often prepare for us, had been rather rough on engineer Joel. You might say it had knocked out a tooth or two and pulled his hair. It had even scarred him a bit.

To carry the analogy further, it was also plain that there had been a blood ceremony. At any rate it seemed to me that the brave blood of Joel's Scandinavian pioneer forebears who had come to the Great Northwest in frontier days still flowed in him. I noticed this every now and then, when in visiting Disney centers of attraction, he began talking about the need for never losing one's creative touch, one's perspective, one's beliefs in life's magic as it expressed itself in Disneyland.

So here we were in a world built upon the Dreaming. As we rode the funicular in and through the grottos of the Matterhorn, I realized in the thrill and wonder of it how closely my feelings must have paralleled the aborigines' response to the Uluru mountain in Arnhem. Gloriously shaken by the rollicking ride, having an illusion that we had gone through the Alps for sure, I recalled the words of adventurer Bill Harney, staunch friend of the aborigines, who said of Uluru, "To most people the ancient mythology of the aboriginals is merely bull and of no account. But as I sit here near Uluru, I remember how the blackfellows read the stories of these stones, of the coming of the Earth Mother which they symbolize, of how she came out of the earth to record the birth of man and his reincarnations. The story of Uluru symbolizes the serpent that is said to revitalize the souls of the people who believe in the cult. I send you greetings from Uluru, from one mountain to another."

Then Joel and I went into the "Haunted Mansion," the nether world where there is no death, only transition, and where life takes on its full dimension of timelessness. Here in this most recent Disney innovation, the Dreaming became fantastic.

The parlor room in which you begin your spooky tour groans and grows to tremendous proportions. Your mundane, everyday world slips away. There is no relevancy now to the things you used to worry about. Your "real life" is suddenly unreal. *The Dreaming* is reality. Now the parlor room slowly sinks into an enchanted bottomless pit. You are walking out through a magically open door and stepping into a tram. You are riding through catacombs where skeletons and spirits grin and giggle and gibber out of coffins and caves. Cold winds strike you and flames flash from fiery fountains while gloriously amazing apparitions come and go with incredible witchery. You are in Dante's *Inferno* and in Milton's *Paradise Regained* at one and the same time. You are living through Swedenborg's *Heaven and Hell,* and it is pure fun and pleasant dreams. Welcome spirit forms are riding with you. They are inviting you to join them in a palatial banquet hall, beautifully haunted and elegantly designed. When you finally step out of the tram and into the light of day, you have been through eternity without having traveled more than several hundred computerized feet of electronic track.

"It's unreally real," I said to Joel. "No matter how many times you make the trip, the effect is more persuasive than anything you can find in spiritualism."

"Perspective!" he exclaimed. "It gives a man a new perspective!"

Such was the case when we boarded the river steamer *The Twain,* named in memory of Mark Twain, and embarked on the make-believe trip around Tom Sawyer's Island. The adventures of Sam Clemens' most famous characters came to life for us as we were confronted by the war whoops of animated Indians, accosted by fearsome fictionized massacre, and reminded by the homemade rafts that we were traveling with Huckleberry Finn on his Mississippi adventure. We went all the way from Missouri to Arkansas just as he did, feeling no disillusionment in the knowledge that we were actually traversing less than a mile and that our paddle wheeler with its big blades splashing ran mechanically on tracks hidden just beneath the surface of the muddy, man-made stream.

Like the aboriginals who in their Dreamtime recalled the legends of their people, so we remembered the folk tales of our youth, the lingering visions that at one time or another find their way into every American heart. Hadn't we always looked and hoped for miracles such as these? Wasn't there something in our culture that spoke realistically of what was represented here in the way of dreams?

A Frontierland where we could take another look at the vaunted creed of law and order. A Jungleland where all the animals were fierce but never to be feared. A "Small World" through which one traveled on an enchanted barque into the customs, music and charm of the world's exotic races. A Storybook Land where the myths and fables come to life and all the characters appear just as we had imagined them to be.

Such was the Dreaming, Disney style, to many an American visitor, reminding us that utopian fantasies never die but continue to move beneath the surface of the sterner stuff of life.

The Dreaming, according to the illiterate but cosmically conscious aborigine, is a process by which an initiate finds rhythm, mystery and the ultimate willingness of nature to reveal its secrets to those worthy of receiving them. To live as one's heroes lived, to become like one's ideal, to be inwardly reborn with the highest attributes of one's beloved ancestors—in that kind of magic the whole idea was to find *oneself.*

It was something more. It was a deep-seated desire not to let the circumstances of life get you down, but to discover the unseen forces which, everywhere in nature, are ready to come to your aid. The boy in the aboriginal culture was made to feel that in the initiatory rites he passed from childhood into manhood, but in the Dreaming he realized this manhood could not be realized unless he also maintained a childlike faith in nature and nature's God.

Small wonder that an authority on the subject, Dr. W. E. H. Stanner of Australia, said, "When the myths about the drama of the Dreamtime are studied with care, it becomes clear that the aborigines have gone far beyond the longest and most difficult step toward the formation of a truly religious outlook. They found in the world about them what they took to be signs of divine intent toward men, and they transformed those signs into assurances of life under mystical nurture. Their symbolic observances toward the signs, in rites and rituals, were in essence acts of faith toward the reliability of that assurance."

Joel began feeling something like this in the *American* dream. As evening came and we started for the gates, he remarked half to himself, "I'm beginning to see things in an altogether different light."

It was then I could feel the closing of the gap between the people who "always were" and we who feel ourselves all too modern and too new. We were finding what the unschooled, untraveled and untrained aborigine found in the Dreaming. For even today, as every scholar of the aborigine knows, the young aboriginals still roam the barren land they love, renewing their affinity with their ancestral world. Without this confidence and without the knowledge that guardian spirits are part of their life, they would be lost indeed.

So it was with Joel. In the magic of the fact that fantasy, properly interpreted, can change one's attitude even though it may not immediately change situations, he was beginning to experience a sense of hope and joy and an overtone of faith.

As we left the grounds to return once more to our own kind of tribal life, the most significant thing he said was, "I wish my wife Marie could have been with us. Just now I don't see anything to worry about. Everything is going to work out okay. Jobs in my field will come back or, if they don't, I'll simply retrain for something else. Marie and I often talked about that, but it never seemed clear or possible until just now. I sure wish she were here."

Eventually we located our car in the overly crowded parking lot, and when we were nicely started on our way, Joel said, "You've never met my wife, have you? I sure wish you could."

"So do I," I agreed. "Send her down sometime and I'll take her to Disneyland."

After all, under the circumstances, what else was I to say?

But magically, back in my mind's eye, I saw a dark-skinned aborigine boy, half-naked and half-free, who might have been Joel or me, wandering thoughtfully in the outback wastes of Arnhem land.

.13.

The Chrysalis

A strange thing happened to me on the way to the post office. I was thinking about butterflies and when I picked up my mail, there was a butterfly letter. Why I should have been thinking along this line I wouldn't know, unless it was the unconscious remembrance of a story I had used in a lecture several nights before—the Chinese legend about the monk who dreamed he was a man playing the role of a butterfly. His dream was so vivid that when he awoke he wondered whether he might now in fact be a butterfly playing the part of a man.

At any rate, there was the letter from a school teacher in Des Moines, Iowa. She had been telling her class of first- and second-graders some stories involving serendipity—a term for those unexpected and fortuitous happenings that seem to come by chance. As one of their projects, her pupils had observed a caterpillar which had wrapped itself in its cocoon, out of which it would eventually emerge as a creature fitted for an altogether new environment. They thought this transformation was in itself amazingly serendiptous.

It dawned on me that to a youngster's mind it might all have seemed like chance. But to us who took pride in our superior wisdom it was destiny, the predetermined pattern in caterpillar life. Caught in its ecological cycle, the crawling creature inevitably arrived at the time when it intuitively prepared its "coffin," sure that its end was near. Yet all the while we, with our infallible knowledge, knew that it was being readied for another life. We named the process "histolysis," and if our earthbound voyager did not know the meaning of the word, no matter.

Of course, the caterpillar may secretly have rebelled against his demise and questioned the reason for it as he felt his brown-green body disintegrate into an amorphous mass. But we wise ones who were in on the secret recognized a cosmic power at work and saw something definitely right with the caterpillar's world, whether he knew it or not. Could there be, I wondered, a Watcher higher than man who looks upon *our* seeming agonies as benignly and with as infinite understanding as we observe the metamorphosis of the larva of a butterfly? If so, there was a good chance of something beyond our knowing being right with *our* world.

Several days later another letter came from the teacher in the midwestern school, advising me that the butterfly had been born. Out of the green egg-shaped chrysalis a golden monarch had emerged. The excited children gave this wisp of life a name: "Monty."

No sooner was it free from its pupal state and out of its cocoon than there was another chrysalis that confined the winged creature—namely, the classroom. The young people decided that while they had little control over its previous confinement, they could exercise some jurisdiction over the present one, and so, on a sparkling autumn afternoon, they opened the window and shooed Monty out into nature's world. With a happy flash of color, he flapped his wings and headed west.

"According to the children," the teacher informed me, "Monty is on his way to California. They are sure he will be appearing in your yard in due time."

Like most adults in California or in any of our fifty booming states, I am a busy man with many interests and with the traditional American urge to live creatively, work incessantly, and travel extensively. Monty had nothing on me. Nonetheless, I could not get him off my mind. I checked with an entomologist about a monarch's cruising speed and learned it was ten-plus miles an hour. That figured out to be a trip of some fourteen days, if all went well and Monty knew the route and flew for twelve hours every day. I thought of him, wherever he might be, during announcements of smog alerts and scorching Santa Ana winds. I hoped his endurance was okay and that the radar and aerodynamic apparatus which heaven had installed within his transparent one-hundredth-ounce body were functioning properly.

While all this bemused me, a gradual dawning of a deeper awareness came over me as I entered into a child's world of thought and wonder. It occurred to me that there were segments in my life which I had unwittingly blocked out as my busy career involved my attention. To be honest, I had to confess that I was literally "cocooned" in my own professional pursuits, wrapped round by a chrysalis of my own making, one which showed no signs of sprouting wings.

There were many of these blocked-out areas, now that I thought about it, but one in particular, made graphic by the story of Monty, was my out-of-touchness with youngsters the age of first- and second-graders. I realized that for years I had seemingly forgotten I had ever been a child, had ever watched in wonder the magic of growing things, believed in miracles, or related to the marvel of life around me.

This was strange, too, because a great deal of my work is with college students. I could level with them all right, and with them I often relived my campus years and saw life through their perceptive eyes. But "grade school" was like something that had never really happened to me.

Parents and grandparents, oddly enough, have confessed to me that they have often had this same remote feeling about that formative period, even with young people literally crawling under their feet. They admitted that they somehow unconsciously stepped over this particular generation, unable or unwilling to identify at a deep level of awareness with a child's world.

Psychoanalyst Carl Jung once had something to say on this in a London lecture. He told his audience that the amazing thing about consciousness is that nothing can be conscious without an ego to which it refers. If something is not related to the ego, it is not conscious. He went on to say that perhaps half of our life is spent in an unconscious condition, and that it is extremely difficult to hold an image of total life because our consciousness is too narrow. We live, as it were, by flashes of existence.

While this may appear to indicate a disconcerting *un*-rightness with the world, it could be one of the most remarkable rightnesses of all if the unconscious is the chrysalis in which, from time to time, new awarenesses are born, new worlds unfold, and new wings are fashioned for our own monarchal flights.

Thinking along these lines, I could not help remembering how a great Teacher once surrounded Himself with a group of children and gave His adult listeners an object lesson in innocence and faith. He went so far as to suggest that heaven belongs to those who can relive the guileless enchantment of their youth.

Some loose ends closed in my estimate of life when I realized that each oncoming generation is another breaking of a chrysalis. In the total ecology of human-kind this is actually a sublime idea, but we lose the point if we fail to see ourselves as part of the pattern. After all, if we feel we have evolved slowly, consider the but-terfly. It certainly did not come into instant existence. The records say that insects existed 250 million years before man appeared on the scene, and that for the first few million years the insects were wingless. This seems to indicate that Whoever was behind the planning was both deliberate and persistent in working toward the world we have today. Think how many bugs and beetles must have felt they never made it, but who nevertheless played their part in the total scheme of things! Man at least has the capability of remembrance if he wishes to use it, and an age of innocence if he cares to recapture it at any time.

So, after several weeks of philosophizing and visualiz-ing Monty doing his thing above the freeway traffic and flapping his wings against the prevailing westerly winds, I received a third mailing from the Des Moines school. The package was large, but the note from the teacher was brief and to the point.

"The enclosed twenty-five letters are from my school family," she said. "They are untouched by teacher's red pencil. I listen and learn from my children. They are sure Monty will come to your house. One pupil said, 'But how will Dr. Bach know which one is Monty?' The answer from another student was, 'Monty will be friendly and gentle and show his love!' "

The treasury of letters, painstakingly printed in pencil on large ruled paper, was magnificently done in thought and deed. Each student expressed his confidence in Monty and embellished his letter with highly colorful bees, butterflies, and flowers.

My temptation was to sit down and sentimentalize a "Dear Children" letter, saying something like: "Your notes to me have closed a gap in my life. Next time I drive the freeways and complain about the traffic I'll think of Monty. Next time life gets me down I'll remember the beautiful things you said. Next time I am looking for something that's right with the world, I'll think of you." And so on.

I checked my romanticizing, wrote a manly acknowledgment and let it go at that.

Yet something has been bothering me, and it will take a bit of doing to decide my next move. If a strange thing happened to me on the way to the post office, an even stranger thing happened one morning when I stepped out onto our patio. There in the sunlight filtering through the eucalyptus trees, I was greeted by the dip of wings and the circumnavigating flight of not one but a veritable swarm of multicolored butterflies— monarchs.

We have a birdfeeder and a birdbath as standard equipment in our flower-bordered yard, but as far as I could remember, I had never noticed a butterfly. Now they were displaying their choreography around the camelia and bougainvillea bushes as if in answer to a special invitation. I invited my wife Lorena to share the scene and assured her that as far as I was concerned, this was more than mere coincidence. It was a pinpoint miracle to see these fragile orange-and-brown visitors fueling up on nectar in our own backyard.

Lorena looked at me in that incredible way women have of making a man's motivations transparent. "What's unusual about it?" she asked in surprise. "We *always* have butterflies around this time of the year."

I insisted that I certainly had never noticed them.

"You may not have noticed them," she agreed, "but they've been around."

"This many?"

"Well, there do seem to be a few additions this morning. It's probably the season."

"Yes," I replied defensively, "and there may just be a delegation from Des Moines, Iowa."

She favored me with a light laugh of understanding as she recalled the correspondence from the school.

"Come now, admit it," I teased. "Think of the thousands of gardens around here. Do you think every yard is alive with monarch butterflies? We should have a picture to prove this."

Since she *is* a camera enthusiast, it was not difficult to persuade her to assemble her equipment for a photographic record. Since hand-holding the Nikon with its telephoto lens was impractical, we mounted the camera on a tripod and focused it on a cluster of bougainvillea blossoms where the butterflies seemed to congregate. Then we attached a long cable release and seated ourselves at the patio table to wait until our subjects assumed a photogenic pose.

While waiting, Lorena decided that a cup of tea would be in order, and she went to the kitchen, leaving me to take the picture if the situation warranted. The rubber bulb of the cable release was within easy reach. I was all set for a butterfly masterpiece as soon as one came within the camera's eye.

Not only did *one* settle on the bougainvillea almost

immediately, but three monarchs posed themselves on the colorful cluster. It was my great moment, but just as I reached out to squeeze the rubber bulb, something happened. A beautiful monarch deliberately landed on the bulb and perched there as if to deliver a special message. Lorena, emerging from the house, saw the cluster of three and exclaimed: "Snap it! Snap it!"

"Can't you see the bulb?" I whispered. "It's Monty!"

By this time the neatly posed trio had flown away, but Monty stayed long enough for us to marvel at his poise and courage. When he finally fluttered away, Lorena said with a sigh, "This morning we should have had *two* cameras."

"It was Monty all right," I assured her. "Didn't the kids say he would be friendly and gentle and show his love?"

"Funny thing," Lorena said. "I remember calling your attention to our butterflies a year ago, and you never even noticed them."

"It's hard for a man to see anything if he's in a cocoon," I confessed.

She took a deep breath of the scented air, poured the tea, and said, "It's going to be a beautiful day."

.14.

The Gloria Patri

Sadie was a lady. The fact was impressed upon me when she tiptoed haughtily off her nest as if she were queen of the sandpipers. Small, gray-white, head erect, eyes alert, she moved proudly through the green tufts of beach grass on the shores of Kootenay Lake.

I stood stock still. She hopped up on a dried-out log which lay among the jumble of rocks in the morning sun. She stood there, teetering rhythmically as sandpipers do, then paced back and forth, challenging me with her indignant high-pitched "Beep-beep."

It may have been a disturbing encounter for her, but for me it was a moment of rightness with the world. After fifteen summers of cabin living in the British Columbia Kootenays, after hearing the "Beep-beep" whenever I came down to the lake, I had finally become a bird watcher, enchanted by the sight and sound of the sandpiper species called *Least*. My recently purchased bird book told me that their habits were "quite tame, occasionally allowing close approach," and that they had "buffy neck and breast, thin bill, sharp eyes, spindly legs, and a voice that said *peep* or *beep,* also a short *k-kreep.* "

Nothing was said about the teetering motion or the white rump bopping up and down, synchronized with the high-pitched beeping. And nothing was said about Sam, the name I had given to Sadie's mate, who, as I stood and watched Sadie, was sitting where he usually sat, on a half-submerged rock close to the water's edge. Slightly larger than Sadie, Sam teetered too, and then flew in dipping, sweeping motions, skimming the water at a feather's length, beeping warnings to his mate and assuring her that he was near at hand.

It was Sam who was responsible for my discovery of Sadie's hideaway. Several weeks ago when I went down to check on the boat, Sam started an unusually excited chatter the moment I appeared. His arpeggio signals clamored for my attention, but as I looked away from him I noticed his partner gliding through the undergrowth. The only way to discover a sandpiper's nest is to spy the mother bird slyly stealing away. The concealment and camouflage of the nest are indescribably perfect. Twigs and grass, scrounged from the locale, are woven into a saucer-sized shape, almost impossible to detect. But if you spot a sandpiper scurrying along the ground, you can depend on it that she has just come from her expertly concealed habitat.

Sadie's nest was tucked against the fragile stems of a foot-high cluster of beach sage in the midst of flat, blue flagstones. It held four spotted, clay-colored eggs, dead ringers for the pebbles on the beach.

Day after day I went down to check on this precious clutch. Whenever the sun was right, my wife Lorena got Sadie into the range of her cameras while I tape-recorded the "Beep-beep" variations. We were determined to get an audio-visual documentary of the birth of Sadie's brood.

We set up a blind—a pup tent some ten feet from the nest—propped the tripod four feet from the eggs, attached a remote cable release to the camera and tried to convince Sadie and Sam that we had no predatory intentions. The longer we watched, the greater became our realization that we were not only observing the characteristics of two shore-line birds, but were being introduced to that Something within nature which in an incomprehensible way endows its creatures with an uncanny instinct and an intelligence that argue strongly for a purposive universe. "A bird," Emerson once said, "is to be seen not in ounces and inches, but in its relations to nature." That was what we were beginning to discover.

There was not only the wonder of the nest itself and the four camouflaged eggs which, according to the bird book, had been laid one a day. There was the matter of Sadie keeping these eggs at the proper 76-degrees for incubation. The sun's heat, the cold of the wind, the pelting rains, all were registered in Sadie's built-in computer.

For weeks we watched and photographed, enticed by the drama unfolding on this tiny spot of our planet Earth. On excessively hot days, Sadie went dutifully to the edge of the lake, waded in and returned to the nest immediately so that her cool, moistened body would restore the eggs to just the right temperature. She did this as if every motion was a divine command. Her haughty walk, the spark of her eyes, the assuring "Beep-beep" whenever she approached the nest as if to advise the unborn chicks that all was well, closed a gap between us and nature's world.

When the rains came she spread her wings to form a protecting watershed. On cool, normal days she was off the nest for such long periods—sometimes for an hour or two—that we waited with trepidation. The sound of a hawk, the flash of a swift moving marten, the chatter of a squirrel, all were threats to the life that pulsed inside the fragile shells. Once Sadie was gone so long we were afraid that something tragic had happened to her. Sam, too, was nowhere to be seen. Moments dragged by. Hours passed, but eventually we heard the faint, familiar sound, "Beep-beep," and saw the teetering bird warily approaching her domain.

Then from the water's edge Sam spaced his "beeps" to convey whatever message he had in mind. Sadie shuffled into the nest, snuggled over the eggs and assured her mate that all was well.

Lorena and I were becoming hopelessly, or hopefully, involved in this maternal interlude. What was happening before our eyes represented a heartbeat of the universe and an inner rightness about the world. I called off business appointments. I explained to guests that the drama being enacted on the beach had a priority which we hoped they would understand. I doubt whether anyone realized or whether we wanted them to know how deeply the lure of the Unseen had gotten hold of us, or how the "Least" among the sandpipers was teaching us a lesson in the role of Nature's laws of love and life.

Day by day Sadie and Sam staged their command performance, filling us with hope and fear as we watched, cramped in the pup tent, straining our eyes, letting time and tide go by, while our obedient shorebirds played their instinctive parts. No matter what was happening in the world of men or what frightening headlines appeared in the daily press, their show went on. Sadie was a lady guided by a cosmic force. Her inborn impulse to bring to life this something of herself was coded in her mind and determined her behavior though waves pounded the shore or north winds blew or lightning flashes broke the Kootenay sky.

Sadie became one of the most photographed mothers in the Kingdom of the *Least.* Lorena's camera caught her entering the nest, exiting, turning the eggs with a wriggle of her body, and showing us an amazing gamut of expressions from boredom to annoyed amusement.

On the morning of the twenty-fourth watchful day, a Sunday morning, I checked on Sadie at the crack of dawn. The sun was just beginning to filter through the pines. A sinister stillness hung over the Kootenay shores. Not even Sam made a sound, nor was he in sight. As I reached the bottom of the stone steps leading to the beach, the raucous scream of a crow challenged our woodland world. A brown squirrel screeched wildly in a tree.

"You did protect her?" I said half-aloud to Nature. "You wouldn't let anything happen to Sadie now!" And I found myself running in the direction of the nest.

"Sadie, Sadie!" I called wordlessly. There was no sound. In my confusion I seemed to have lost sight of the nest's location. "Sadie! Sadie!" I said aloud.

Then I saw her, standing alert and alone, teetering beside the nest, oblivious of me, oblivious of everything except this moment in time, this moment and a thought, whatever the thought may have been. Or could it be that she had been waiting for me, waiting to show me the incredible magic of birth and life?

It was almost, as though she *had* wanted me to come, for now she began to beep, meantime pecking ever-so-lightly at an egg as if to make an indentation. There was an immediate response, an almost imperceptible movement of the egg, than a sudden breaking of the shell and the gradual emergence of a fuzzy hatchling whose wet miniature wings seemed to sprout and dry as the globule of life shook itself and undertook a first uncertain step on its tiny toothpick legs.

Sadie stood beside the nest, every inch a queen. Her "beep-beep" changed into a song which might for all the world have been the melodious singing of a meadowlark. Liquid and clear, her bubbling melody announced her firstborn to the world while she stood teetering over the valiantly unsteady object at her feet.

Suddenly she stopped her song. Impulsively she seized one half of the broken eggshell in her beak and flew off with it, returning immediately for the other half. Why did she do this? I had observed other birds, robins, for example, unconcerned about the eggshells in their nest. I had found abandoned nests with broken shells still in them after the birds had gone. Sadie was different. She had taken away this hatched-out egg as if in answer to an inner command. Now she crouched over the nest shielding the wriggling chick and keeping the other eggs warm and vital for their miraculous moment of birth.

The photographic climax we had waited for was now at hand. I rushed up to the cabin to summon Lorena with her cameras and to bring my tape recorder in the hope of picking up Sadie's indescribable song.

The timing was perfect. When Lorena and I got back "on location," the second hatchling was magically emerging from its broken shell and there was Sadie teetering and intoning her incredible *Gloria Patri.* As if she didn't mind, almost as if for our benefit, she sang her song while I recorded it on tape and Lorena's camera caught the wonder of the singer in a scene exceedingly rare on film or tape. Then, once more, impulsively, almost excitedly, Sadie flew off with a piece of eggshell just as the third egg broke open and another tiny throb of life appeared. Lorena, standing almost over the nest, got a close-up of the breaking of this shell. We could see the tiny index lines increase as the chick's activity inside broke open the clay-white chrysalis. The moist form emerged slowly, gropingly, but seeking almost at once to test its spindly legs.

The firstborn was actually standing now, teetering unsteadily, emitting its first faint *"Beep."* Sadie was deeply involved in protecting her three chicks, getting rid of the eggshells, warming the last remaining egg, and doing justice to the glory of her song as if somewhere Sam were waiting.

Time passed swiftly for us, and perhaps for Sadie too, for the hatchlings seemed to grow with every passing moment, and they were already venturing from the nest. But now something happened. Although we had gone into our blind we could hear an uncertainty in Sadie's song and see it in her perplexed expression as she eyed the last remaining egg. Almost as if to ask, "Why doesn't it hatch?" she divided her time between concern for it and a concentrated effort to keep the three fledglings under her at the nest until the remaining egg hatched.

We watched and wondered; as time went by Sadie permitted the trio to test their legs and walk and teeter and emit their intermittent beeps in answer to her calls. It was mid-day now and Lorena said, "That last egg isn't going to hatch. By now it must be cold."

An hour later, after Sadie had taken her three sandpiperettes some distance from the nest and was teaching them how to forage for food, we bent over the nest to examine the reluctant umber-spotted egg Now we could see a tiny pinpoint of beak protruding through the shell. Around the egg, no larger than the trace of a well-sharpened pencil, an irregular line could also be seen. Lorena peered at it closely, then exclaimed, "I see what's happened!" She picked up the egg and gently removed a half of a previously discarded eggshell that had accidently become encased over this remaining egg. Evidently this had taken place during the excitement of the three nearly simultaneous births. This sheath, forming a double wall, made it impossible for the unborn chick to break out and made it equally impossible for Sadie to effectively peck through so as to release it. The desperate attempt of the unborn chick to peck its way out had lodged its beak in this vise-like covering.

Now we understood why Sadie had flown away with each eggshell the moment a bird was hatched. It was not to throw predators off the scent, as we had surmised, but rather to keep a tragedy of the kind we were witnessing from happening. Perhaps while she was taking a piece of shell away, she accidently caused the other half to slip over this final egg. Her bewilderment at this was understandable and her final frustration when she gave up and walked away could now be understood.

Now that Lorena had carefully slipped the sheath of shell off the egg, we hoped against hope that the chick inside could still hatch. Replacing the egg and the piece of shell separately in the nest, we went back to our blind and waited. Sadie came back almost immediately. This time she flew directly to the nest. Impulsively she seized the broken eggshell and flew away with it. Then she came back, stood for a moment, teetering, on the edge of the nest. We watched her as she eyed the egg thoughtfully, hopefully.

I wondered whether I was reading her thoughts as the idea came to me that she was inquiring into the mystery of all this, trying to piece together the puzzle of life—and death. Was she blaming herself, or fate? Was she more grateful that three chicks had seen the light of day than remorseful over one that had died?

We would never know, but as we watched, we saw her fluff her wings as if to close the chapter on this inexorable happening. Then with an air of superb fatalism, she emitted a resigned "Beep-beep" and strutted off to join her brood of three who were making their stumbling, eager way into the world of sticks and stones on Kootenay beach.

By midafternoon the hatchlings were steady on their spindly, yellowish legs, teetering and beeping. At dusk they responded to Sadie's calls of "Follow me." By early evening they were well on their way to a migratory life while Sam was showing off in capers over the water's edge.

We removed the egg from the nest and found the beak of the unborn chick still embedded in the shell. The following morning when we returned to the spot, either Sadie or Sam had flattened out the nest, leaving the premises with scarcely a sign that a miracle of love and birth and resignation had taken place in this pinpoint area of God's world.

As I have said, all I ever knew about sandpipers was that they said "Beep-beep," and that they teetered, but this was only because I had never seen them in their moment of creation when, for a little while, they sang their secret songs. I have a hunch there is a lesson in this having to do not only with our relationship with birds but with the total family of mankind as well.

At any rate, a queenly sandpiper on a beach taught

us a rare lesson in persistency and perseverance. Loneliness, meaninglessness and the unknown may, as someone has said, be three kinds of fear in human life. But in the example of Sadie, something told us there are also three kinds of faith: courage, commitment, and obedience to some inner divine command, making everything that happens somehow right with the world.

.15.

The American

Among things truly right with the world are rare individuals like H. J. B. There must be others like her in other lands scattered around planet Earth, seedlings of something selfless and good, and there can be little doubt that their presence makes and keeps their countries great.

H. J. B. happens to be an American, but I heard about her in Yamashina, Japan, where I had as my interpreter the Japanese scholar Colbert Kurokawa. During our travels he told me that when his personal library was destroyed by fire a Mrs. H. J. B., living in Ames, Iowa, heard about his loss and began replenishing his books. This unexpected gesture of friendship caused Kurokawa to look upon all Americans with greater affection.

In Detroit, Michigan, I met one of the state's leading dietitians, Armesia Lloyd. She informed me that in the 1930's when Negroes were barred from living in dormitories on the Ames campus, a white woman whom she affectionately referred to as H. J. B. invited her to live in her home. "I owe her a great debt," said Mrs. Lloyd, "not only for taking me in as a member of the family, but for making real the American dream."

I heard a similar story in Honolulu when I talked with Hawaiian-born Barbara Matsuura, counselor in the Oahu schools. In the mid-sixties Barbara came to Ames from her plantation home in Kahuka, hoping to go to college. At the airport she met a buoyant, rosy-cheeked housewife who was welcoming another student. "She must have sensed my loneliness," Barbara explained. "She came to me and said, 'Until you find your way around, why not stay with me?' Her home became my home and she was like a second mother to me. Often in my counseling I am guided by what I learned from H. J. B."

When A. V. Suraweera, a professor in Ceylon, was awarded an Asian Foundation grant for work at the State University of Iowa in Iowa City and found it next to impossible to locate a place to stay, a friend of his in Ceylon persuaded him to write to a woman in Ames who had befriended him. Though Iowa City is 120 miles from Ames, H. J. B. took on the assignment and wrote Professor Suraweera to come along. He replied gratefully—adding, however, that not only was he coming to America but so were his wife and three children, aged five, seven and nine.

Weeks later, at eleven o'clock at night, H. J. B. received a telephone call. A heavily accented voice said, "We are at the Des Moines airport. Where are you?" The Suraweera family had arrived unannounced, their cablegram having gone astray. H. J. B. drove to Des Moines, picked up the family and transported them to Iowa City where she had completely outfitted a Quonset hut as a home for them. Said Professor Suraweera, "When I am asked what I think of the U.S.A., I think of H. J. B."

My introduction to this woman who makes people's worlds go round came by way of a letter shortly before Christmas.

"I have read one of your books," said the handwrit
ten message, "and I thought it would be a lovely gift
for several people I know. If I asked you real nice,
would you autograph some copies for me?"

The gift list which followed listed seventy-five names,
each with a thumbnail sketch of the intended receiver.
"I thought you might be interested in knowing something about the people," said H. J. B. apologetically.

One book was intended for a taxi driver in Tokyo
who, according to the notation, "Was so kind to me one
day." Another went to a saleswoman in the Philippines:
"She was so helpful." Another was for the Reverend
Mr. Kwankin of Agra, India: "He will enjoy the book
so much." Another went to a merchant in the Middle
East: "He was once so generous to me." College students, acquaintances in Hawaii, all constituted a well-
remembered chain of fellowship around the world.

That might have ended the matter, but for the fact
that after I autographed the books, I received a note
of thanks together with a casual message. "You were
so kind to put such lovely notes in my books; would you
possibly have time to autograph a few more? I know
how busy you must be."

I called a local bookstore to inquire if they had more
of my books. They did. But hardly enough, for H. J. B.
sent seventy-five more names together with biograph-
ical notes and the usual covering check.

Then I met her. An invitation from a group of young
people asked me to speak at the Ames Methodist
Church. They had heard of me by way of H. J. B., whom
they admired very much. When the minister introduced
me at the morning service he took time to say, "We
have literally rolled out the red carpet for you. As you

see, the church has been newly carpeted and the workmen finished the job just last night. The donor wishes to be anonymous."

When my eyes wandered over the congregation I could not help but notice, in the tenth row, a relaxed, vivaciously friendly woman with dimpled cheeks and infectious smile. Somewhat beyond middle-age, she was seated with five serene and elderly worshipers whom, I learned later, she had picked up and brought to the service as she did on many a Sunday morning.

Guests at the dinner in her home after the service included students of various nationalities and a number of townspeople, all enjoying themselves in the homey cottage-type residence on Northwestern Avenue, a place as warm and outward-going as H. J. B. herself. Apparently every one of these people had been influenced and helped somewhere along the way by the unpretentious insight of this ambassador of the American dream. One of the men said, "They say that H. J. B. lives here alone, but everyone who drops in, students particularly, is a member of her family."

Another guest confided, "You could pass this house a hundred times without realizing how the lines of friendship go out all around the world by way of this woman. It is her nature to see the needs of people and help fill those needs, knowing just how far to go to put people on their own responsibility."

I met Elfrieda Stahlhut, an artist with the Hallmark Company in Kansas City. She had come from Germany some twenty years ago to visit relatives on a midwestern farm and to try to find a job in the U.S.A. She had saved her money to make the trip, but became homesick and discouraged. One day she happened to meet H. J. B.

"We went for a walk," Elfrieda recalled, " and she

asked me how I liked America. I told her in my broken English that it was not what I had expected. She said, 'Stay with me for a few days and let me take you around.' That was the turning point in my life. Out of love for a stranger, this busy woman sat down with me night after night and taught me English. She would take me to a store and wait in the car while I went in and struggled with the language until I bought what was needed. I stayed with her for over a year. When she learned that I had studied art in Germany, she enrolled me in art courses at the university. One day she handed me a checkbook, saying it was time I learned how to handle American money. She had opened an account for me. Then came the assignment at Hallmark. When I asked her how I could ever repay her, she said, 'If you have a chance to help someone, do so; that is the best thanks.' "

This was also the suggestion that H. J. B. passed along to an immigrant student, Henry Schwermann, now a practicing veterinarian in New Ulm, Minnesota. When Henry left Ames following his graduation, he asked H. J. B. how he could ever thank her for making his education possible. She said, "If I helped you in any way, perhaps someday you will have the opportunity to do the same for someone else."

Kathryn Hughes, educational specialist for the Federal Extension Service in Washington, D.C., was another of H. J. B.'s protegés. "I received much more than a college education because of her," said Mrs. Hughes. "Not only did I get extra help in my profession, I also got some wonderful training in how to accept life through my association with her."

H. J. B.'s perspective on America was inherited from her Scandinavian parents, who came to the Midwest prior to World War I. With inordinate thrift and a will to work, they bought a small farm near Ames, and through the years they purchased additional acres as finances allowed. Though they were never considered wealthy, they were known for their support of individuals and projects which they felt were deserving. Grateful for the opportunities America had given them, they were foster parents to four young people during the years of the depression.

When H. J. B.'s formal education was interrupted by sickness, she opened a dressmaking service in her home and became sought after by virtue of her skill and the quality of both her work and her character. She married an engineer, and together they took a special interest in the needs of university students.

Then in the space of one year her parents and her husband passed away. The intimate family relationship was abruptly shattered, but H. J. B. met sorrow with remarkable fortitude, a hint of which is noted by a marker over the graves. The Emersonian quotation reads, "Say not, behold an hour of my life is gone, but, rather, I have lived an hour."

As time went by, her activities reached out in ever increasing help to people, always without publicity and usually without mention of her name. The Mary Greeley Hospital in Ames announced that an anonymous giver had renovated some storerooms and transformed them into impressive waiting rooms for parents and children. A woman in a nursing home who felt despairingly that she had been forgotten by relatives and friends regularly received flowering plants with a note saying, "From your neighbors who miss you."

H. J. B. never says, "I bought this for you," or "This is a gift for you," or "Wouldn't you like this?" On the contrary, she puts it this way: "I just happened to have this around," or, "I don't know how I happened to have *two* of these." Not long ago she gave a set of China dishes to a friend with the excuse, "I've used these so long, why don't you use them a while?"

An elderly couple who had no TV set and who had a great deal of pride when it came to accepting charity, received a set from H. J. B. with the excuse that "I am having my rugs cleaned and wondered if you would mind keeping my TV in your home for a while." Obviously, it was never reclaimed.

Assistance to boys' clubs, civic programs, state projects, help to students and people in need were part of an onward-going quiet philanthropy. On one occasion when a $10,000 insurance policy matured, H. J. B. listened to her banker's suggestion that she invest the money in some good, sound stocks or bonds. "That is just what I plan to do," she told him. "I plan to invest it in three young students whose lives and careers will benefit greatly from a trip around the world." Which is what she did.

"How do you thank someone for things like that?" asks Denni Wendell, one of the recipients of the trip, now librarian at Iowa University. "How do you express gratitude to someone who wants to stay out of the picture? When the Hai-O-Hawaii Club wished to present H. J. B. with a milo-mango tray made especially for her, do you think she could be persuaded to come to the meeting? We had to cajole and plead with her and finally tell her how disappointed everyone would be if she did not drop around. Reluctantly she came, as if asking why she should accept any credit when it had all been fun."

Art instructor Gladys Hamlin of Iowa University believes that H. J. B.'s Scandinavian father with his deep and abiding love for his adopted land was responsible for the "Americanization" of H. J. B. She remembers him as a homespun philosopher with an affection for the land and a mystical insight into nature. Many of his sayings became texts-to-live-by for H. J. B. For example, "There may be short-cuts to living, but whatever you do, do it so that it will stand the test of time." "It is very well to work hard and make money, but remember there are many different kinds of banks. There is the bank of good deeds and good living and help to others. Be sure to make substantial deposits in these banks, too."

H. J. B. relates how she once accompanied her parents to an art gallery. Later, while driving in the country, she noticed an old broken gate covered with flowers that reminded her of a picture in the gallery. Her father said, "If you keep your eyes open you will see more pictures in nature in a day than you will in an art museum in a lifetime."

Not long ago H. J. B. unassumingly enlisted the aid of an artist, a writer and a photographer to prepare a prestige book on *The Sculpture of Fred and Mabel Torrey.* The Torreys are American artists whose Lincoln statutes are found in the Art Institute, Chicago, at Millikin University, on the capital grounds in Des Moines, Iowa, and elsewhere in the United States. H. J. B. was convinced that the life and work of the Torreys, protegés of Lorado Taft, should be brought to the attention of young Americans.

No one knows how many replicas of *Lincoln and Tad* she has presented to schools and to individuals. I know of one that resides in a jungle church in Africa whose minister had been inspired by Lincoln's life and thought. She unobtrusively gave another to an elementary school in Des Moines because the children there had known and loved the Torreys.

As I have said, there must be H. J. B.'s in many countries, selfless individuals who represent the building blocks of something instinctively right with the world. In our good days we remember the interplay of these people upon our lives; and in some of our better, higher moments we, too, because of them, are challenged to do a bit more to keep the wheels of the world turning more rightly for others and for ourselves.

.16.

The Gannets

I used to have a theory that people's behavioral patterns are so thoroughly fixed after middle age that they cannot be reprogrammed. They may change *within* the pattern, I insisted, but the pattern does not change. Then I met Penelope O'Hare.

When I first saw her in a Sydney, Australia camera shop near closing time one evening, she was buying a sizable quota of film and fretfully searching for her coin purse inside her cluttered handbag. Finally she dumped the contents of the bag on the glass showcase.

"There," she exclaimed, dramatically extending helpless hands over the disarray, "that's the picture of my life. That's what things have been like ever since I left California, and even before that!"

My preconception about behavioral patterns was reconfirmed. This well-groomed, attractive woman, I told myself, was hung up on self-pity and wrapped round by self-centeredness, a direct extension of conditioned responses. Here she was—fortyish, I judged her to be, luxuriously blonde-haired, obviously interesting if she would only recognize and play up her pleasing qualities, but no doubt it was already too late. The preconscious pattern was too deeply fixed.

To verify my theory, I engaged her in conversation. This was easy, since I too was from California, and we both had Leica cameras strung over our shoulders. She was diffident at first, but while waiting for her purchases to be packaged she got the impression that I had a counselor's ear for people with problems like hers. That was true, and I may have encouraged the impression. But an hour later I was convinced someone might better have counseled *me*, because I invited her to dinner and soon found myself sitting across from her at a table in the Gazebo Hotel.

At that, the whole thing could have had the making of an interesting evening, but for the fact that I was not in the mood to handle a psycho-analytical session or to listen to a tiringly long dissertation on what was wrong with the world according to Penelope O'Hare.

Her bill of complaints was by no means new, and her list of grievances was hardly innovative. Recently divorced after twenty-two years of married life, she felt she was also losing the love of her sixteen-year-old daughter, enrolled in a private school in California. Her son, who had served in Vietnam, had, according to her view, been morally corrupted by drugs in a morally indefensible war.

"But," she assured me, leaving her food untouched and impatiently waiting for another Martini, "it is not just a personal matter, it is a *world* matter. The whole world is in such a state that even if a person *wants* to live right and do the right thing, it is quite impossible."

As the meal ended she submitted her own clinical observation that her biggest problem was *people*. Something dreadful had happened to people. Proof of what she was saying was irrefutable, she assured me, and all I had to do was listen to her account of what happened to her when she joined the photographic tour that started her on this South Pacific trip. The tour leader had been very nice, but the *people,* twenty of them, should never have been assembled without a thorough screening. She had left the group in disgust when they reached Fiji. Any lone woman who travels with a tour party, she averred, must be out of her mind. Now she was on her own and could take pictures when and where she pleased and for as long as she pleased without being "part of the herd."

So the evening passed, and four weeks went by, and Penelope O'Hare was little more than a memory. I had no expectation of ever seeing her again. But one day in Auckland, New Zealand, when I was passing through the crowded lobby of the Royal International, I caught sight of a camera-laden tourist registering at the desk. A sequence of images triggered the thought, "Isn't that So-and-So whom I met in Sydney? What was her name? Penelope O'Hare?"

It was—and it wasn't.

Proof of some kind of transformation was relayed when she looked around, saw me, modestly raised her hand and smiled. I went over to say hello and thought for a moment something must have happened to *me* as I felt the warm response that came over me when she extended her hand. She was sun-tanned and radiant. Casually dressed, she gave the impression of being perfectly relaxed and confident, completely in command of herself.

Her words were pleasantly positive when she said, "It is so good to see you again."

"You look wonderful," I told her.

"I've had a most wonderful time," she assured me.

"I can see you did. You must have met just the right people."

"Just right," she agreed and started to leave. Hesitating a moment, she ventured, "By the way, I have often thought about our dinner together." She smiled and gave her words a light touch. "It seems like such a lifetime ago."

"It occurs to me," I found myself saying, "that it was four weeks, almost to a day."

"Don't have too good a memory about that, will you?" she added wistfully but with a serious note.

"That dinner," I had to say, "must definitely have been with someone else, not you."

"Thank you," she said.

She pressed my hand and walked away.

Curiosity and a feeling at a deeper level prompted me to get in touch with her by calling her room the following day. It took a bit of doing to get her to accept an evening dinner date. Actually she was leaving late that night for the States. She had been in touch with both her daughter and her son, and was looking forward to seeing them in Hawaii.

The reasons behind the transformation of Penelope O'Hare, however, had nothing to do with her children. It had to do with gannets in the stark and barren cliffs off New Zealand's north island, a promontory called "Cape Kidnappers"; jutting out into the sea, the largest and most spectacular gannetry of the South Pacific.

These incredible migratory birds are white in color, goose-like in size, with wing spans of five to six feet and head crowned with gold. To study and photograph them, people are willing to brave the six miles of soggy beach, walking watchfully between the swaying ocean on one side and on the other towering walls of rock and clay which wind and water have carved into awesome shapes. Here one ventures at low tide knowing that there is no escape if the tide comes in or if a storm should lash the sea.

The tour folder which Penelope had carried with her since she left what she had called "the herd" in Fiji, said, "Photograph 100,000 Gannets in their Native Habitat!"

The lure of the challenging invitation possessed her, and since she "didn't like people," she decided to make the trip alone, flying first to Napier, a seaport town facing the Pacific. Napier boasted that "There is no land between us and South America 8,000 miles away." Napier had a motto, "Faith and Courage."

So Penelope flew to Napier where she stayed overnight in a motel, having ordered a taxi to pick her up at five in the morning and take her to Clifton, the starting point for the trek to Cape Kidnappers and the gannet sanctuary. She could have taken a bus later in the day, but that would have meant people, tourists.

The motel manager cautioned her about the six-mile walk and the possibility of rain and bad weather, but she shrugged him off. Did a person need to be in training to walk six miles? Of course, six miles *to* the sanctuary and six miles back, twelve miles, carrying cameras and gadget bag, was quite a trip, but she felt she knew her capabilities.

So she went to bed studying the guide book and the map which assured her she was in romantic country, Maori country, with unpronounceable towns: Te Away, Awatoto, Haumoana, Waichiki, Whakutu. She made a point of this while telling me the story because it dawned on her for the first time, in reading the exotic-sounding names, that the world was greater and more complex than she had ever imagined. Rarely had she thought about the world in this way. Now, alone in the night silence of her motel room, on the verge of what to her was a new adventure, she told herself that in every corner of the globe there are strange-sounding names. On every map are cities and villages and mountains and streams that someone calls "home." Everywhere, apparently, someone has something and someone to love.

But what interested and impressed her most was the information-folder insight into the life-style of the gannets: "The gannet is very much of an individualist, yet it nests in large numbers as if seeking protection from natural enemies. The nest spacing is determined by the pecking range of the bird on the nest, who will attack any object or other bird which strays into its territory. It is an individualist, but one who apparently recognizes his sociological relationship with life."

She re-read these lines in her motel room until she fell asleep.

The morning for her adventure was cold and damp with a threat of rain. The motel manager, who called her at four-thirty and who had packed a lunch for her, again asked her to reconsider going out on such a poor day for photography, but she suspected he was really doubting her ability to make the trip.

The taxi driver, too, expressed concern for her. She interpreted this as his scheme for wanting to be her guide. She made it clear that he need not return for her, since a Land Rover was scheduled to arrive at Cape Kidnappers in late afternoon. This vehicle was mechanically equipped for the rugged drive and worked under a franchise which permitted it to get close to gannet territory. With this in mind, she was protecting herself against the six-mile return trip if she did not care to make the trip both ways on foot.

So the taxi driver took her to the end of the road at Clifton and watched her as she determinedly left the cab to make her way to the office of the Bird Sanctuary

Board at Domain Camp. Here she applied for permission to enter the access route along the tidal beach. As the ranger wrote out the permit, he cautioned her about the tide time, the winds, the trail; warned her against attempting to wander off the prescribed route; and impressed upon her the danger of rocks falling from the cliffs on such a windy day. He did not doubt her ability or her right to make the trip alone, but felt prompted to point out the fact that the Board could not be responsible for any risk or accident during her day-long stay.

It was now approximately six A.M. and well within the prescribed hour for starting the trip. The best time to reach the Sanctuary and return, said the instructions, is not earlier than three hours after high tide and not later than four hours *before* high tide, all conditions subject to weather, wind and waves.

In telling the story she confided to me that less than ten minutes after leaving the Domain Office, she felt a sense of aloneness never experienced in the forty-five years of her sheltered life. Lonely she had been to be sure, and forsaken many times, but there had always been some sign of man-made life around her. She had never before wandered out of sight of houses or fields or highways or city streets. She had been on ocean beaches many times, but always within reach of "civilization." She had often heard the sound of the surf, but always there had been boats on the water or wharves and piers to indicate that humanity was not far away. Now, for the first time in her life, she was where no mortal had seemingly ever been before or left as much as a reassuring footprint in the sands.

For once she was alone with sea and sky and cliffs that grew increasingly more voiceless and challenging. If only the sun were shining, she thought. If only the moan of the wind could be stilled. The sea itself sang a dirge to the brooding clouds, and there was nothing to speak, any living presence—no bird, no plane, not even a sign of limpet life as one might expect on beaches anywhere.

As she walked, the cliffs stretched higher. The expanse of sky spoke impellingly of space, and she remembered how Napier boasted of looking out across 8,000 miles of water between shore and shore. If a person were caught between the rising tide and the wall of rock it was true, there would be no escape.

Her cameras, gadget bag, her lunch package stuffed into her auxiliary pouch became heavy and exhausting. Her raincoat was oppressively hot. She was both hot and cold. Her scarf tied under her chin was suddenly uncomfortable as if holding her captive. She took it off and let the wind blow her hair and then found the sudden feeling of untried freedom frightening. She was tempted to turn back but now, almost an hour's walk from the ranger station, it seemed foolhardy to return and admit fear or, even worse, to confess she had been wrong about her capabilities.

Anxiety, fear, apprehension. She could not easily shake them off. Yet what could happen? Her timing, as far as the tide was concerned, was accurate enough. For once she was free of "people." Not actually physically tired, in an attempt to reassure herself she put down her cameras and took off her raincoat. For an instant a sense of exhilaration came over her. She stood tall, took a deep breath and tried to imagine herself part of the scene around her. Suddenly the reality of freedom was frightening. "My God," she whispered to herself as she stood there, "how alone I really am! If something happened to me, who would know and who would care?"

The lines she had read and re-read the previous night went through her mind: *"The gannet is very much of an individualist, yet it nests in large numbers as if seeking protection from natural enemies. . . . It is an individualist, but one who apparently recognizes his sociological relationship with life."*
She did not know whether to laugh or cry. The world —either world, nature's or man's—was a mystery. How could anyone feel at home in it if he so much as challenged it or ventured to change his environment? All she knew was that she had to go on. Somewhere in a photographic journal she had read that camera enthusiasts often forget that some of the best pictures are taken when the sun is obscured, and some of the most memorable photos are those taken at inopportune and unexpected times.

She steadied her camera on a rock jutting from the sand and took several shots of the ocean and the angry clouds. Then she studied her access map. At this point it occurred to her that those who had shown concern for her actually *did* have her safety in mind. Was there, she wondered, a rightness in the world that she had misinterpreted and perverted by her own suspicions?

Realizing that her camera could not encompass the whole wide screen of sky and water, she began to concentrate on seeing the small, minuscule objects on the beach. She had an impulse to walk barefooted and stuffed her shoes and socks into her gadget bag. The damp sand was hardly comfortable or enjoyable as it might have been on a sunny, pleasanter day, and a sense of depression came over her.

A remembrance from her girlhood, of running carefree and unafraid on a public beach, set echoes reverberating in her mind. "What have I lost? Can I blame it on the world? Is it really the fault of others?"

She walked on, wishing for someone, anyone, a human being like herself, someone to talk to, to walk with. She found herself thinking about God and saying to herself, "He must have something to do with all this, the cliffs, the ocean, the clouds and me."

Looking back, she saw the pattern of her footprints in the sand, an uneven contour, as uncertain as her thoughts. When she proceeded on her way she came upon a dead bird lying with wings outspread, almost as if in flight. It was larger than a gull, gray-white, its head tucked beneath its body as if hiding itself from the world had been its final act.

She confessed to me that at this point she could hardly understand her sense of self-control. The sight of the bird, instead of upsetting her, caused her to wonder dispassionately what had caused its death. Was it a victim of misjudgment as it dove for food into the sea? Had it done battle with another bird, was it a victim of man's pollution, or had it simply fulfilled its life purpose and come here to die and be washed away in the tide?

It was later, an hour or more, as she leaned against a fallen boulder, that the fear she had suppressed swept over her. An overwhelming weariness, a sense of useless futility converged on her. The tangled interweaving of circumstances, her lack of direction for the future were as hopeless as the ashen sky. "Why not admit it?" she told herself aloud, "you *are* literally caught between the sea and the cliffs. The tide could come in. You have lost track of time."

Although it was hours since her last meal, she had no desire to eat. Instead she walked on, closing in upon herself more and more even as the access route now converged on her. In the distance she could see the outline of the black reef and the rocky chimney-like formations on which the gannets were supposed to be found. It was still a mile away, but the guide book said there was a rest hut which would serve as a welcome stop even though it was unattended and as lonely as the cliffs themselves.

She walked on. Then, just as she spied a cluster of trees in the distance she heard the metallic scream of a bird. A gannet, the first she had seen, lifted itself with effort from a distant cliff. Once in the air it shot upward as if caught by a funnel of wind. Its giant wings spreading strongly against the clouds provided a picture impressively beautiful. Its perfect command in flight, its warning cry as if to alert the colony to the presence of a human being, its choreography over the water, filled Penelope with a sudden sense of power and confidence in herself.

What thrilled her even more was a ray of sunlight breaking through the overcast and touching the white wings and yellow hood of the gliding bird. Breathlessly she watched, disinclined even to attempt a picture. Alone, more alone than she had ever been, she was now conscious of a multipresence as if supported by everyone who might conceivably have sometime shared a similar scene.

Somewhere between rejection and acceptance, between fear and a sense of transcendence, she found an integrated self which until this moment had eluded her. Between conflicting impulses of pity for herself and a surge of power, she saw for a transfigured moment the person she really was or the one she felt she had the capacity to become.

Thoughtfully she attached a telephoto lens to her camera and made her way to a nearby vantage point not far from the black reef. Her feeling of exhaustion was gone. Her sense of fear had left her. She was strangely at home in an incredible universe where the clouds were actually breaking as if her changed mood had influenced even the weather.

Within the camera lens she caught her first glimpse of a covey of gannets rising from the reef. Getting them into range, she began photographing them excitedly as they circled in exhilarating flight. They floated in the murmur of the wind, then flew swiftly to a great height where they performed their acrobatics with the thrill of freedom.

She focused on one whose wings were lustrous in the sunlight. She could catch flashes of his golden hood. But suddenly when she had him, her prize subject, in sharp focus, he plunged without warning straight down into the sea at rocket-speed.

The plummeting bird was like a lightning flash. It hit the water at a speed that sent it instantly out of sight. It was a suicidal plunge, and for a moment Penelope wondered whether this was how the bird had died whose body she had seen stretched out on the beach. But now the gannet which had taken the awesome leap reappeared phoenix-like upon the water, a small fish triumphantly clutched in its serrated beak.

Penelope stood motionlessly in tears. Never had she witnessed anything so dramatic. It was as if the gannet had unfolded the total role of nature and life just for her. The fish, inescapably captive; the proud bird raising its powerful body gallantly with its catch, skimming the water, muscular wings flapping; the sun, the sea, the opening sky were telling her that there is meaning in life and death beyond one's knowing. There are worlds in motion which one never sees, dramas being played

without spectators, life being lived in cycles never realized unless one is privileged to be a witness to something universal.

Any feeling of doubt about her reason for having
come on this venture vanished. Above the summit of
the great reef, scores of gannets were soaring. They
lured her on as she made her way up a steep trail which
rose from the beach. The rest hut was by-passed. She
climbed on with an ever new reserve of strength and
soon crossed the point of land where, for once, she was
looking down upon the sand and the sea. She was above
it all now, above the beach and the tide.

An unforgettable scene confronted her when she
reached the top of the reef. Here lay the gannet rookery
with its thousands of birds, nesting pair by pair on their
mounds, their marked-out territory, a colony intimate
yet individualized. Here they were, hardly mindful of
the presence of a lone human being, secure in a knowledge of mutual protection.

At first she feared she might disturb this crowded
gannet city. Then it flashed through her mind how
helpless she would be if they suddenly converged on
her. The thought came and went. She felt secure. Adjusting her camera she began focusing on pairs, then
on individual birds as they turned their eggs with their
sharp beaks, rearranged strips of seaweed in their nests,
preened their feathers, stretched their wings, posed for
her and flew in free formations overhead.

In relating this to me she said that the key word was
"identity," identity with all life. From the courageous
bird which did its disappearing act into the sea in search
for food, to the fish fated for capture; from the gannets
who defended their nesting mounds to those who re-

laxed in seeming enjoyment of colony living, identity was involved in the realization that her own relationship to life was changing.

Picture taking was part of the identification process as the hours passed. No longer a spectator watching a performance, she had a sense of belonging. Everything that had happened to her at every period in her existence was now part of a cosmic feeling that everything was right and part of a good destiny. What convinced her most of all that a change had taken place in her was the fact that she saw the tide rising, cutting off her way to return, and she was not afraid. The Land Rover which was supposed to come was nowhere in sight. She was alone and the sun was beginning to set; yet she had no fear and continued photographing the gannets against the changing sky.

I had been annoyed with Penelope O'Hare's complaints about the frustrations in her world; now I was frustrated by her bemused reluctance to go into detail about how she had returned from gannet country. Cape Kidnappers is an isolated place, and after all, she was there when night began to fall, with no sign of transportation in sight. After some questioning, she explained that the Land Rover had broken down and it was dark when it finally reached the gannetry. The driver, who had eventually spotted a camera-laden woman walking fearlessly along the trail, was reported to have said that he could not imagine anyone being that calm under the circumstances.

"So that is how you got back to Napier," I said. "I thought perhaps the gannets picked you up and flew you back."

She looked at me as if we were communicating for the first time.

"They did pick me up, you know," she mused. "Did you know that gannets born on the reef, though they have never flown, instinctively rise up at the appointed time for migration and fly seventeen hundred miles without any previous experience in either flight or direction-finding? They simply take off, arriving at their new home across the Tasman Sea fully equipped to meet life as it is made to be lived in nature's world."

"The gannet," the guide book said, "is very much of an individualist . . . but one who apparently recognizes his sociological relationship with life." Which, in itself, is quite an insight into our discovery of something challenging and right in the world of all mankind.

.17.

The Toll Road

Recently I experienced another of my periodic conversions to quietude. This happens quite often; I promise myself that I will change the tempo of my life from *vivo* to *andante* or shift the composition of my days from *allegro* to *dolce.* At such times I look at the world around me as if I were an appalled spectator unwilling to believe I am actually a part of it and determined never again to be caught in its maddening orchestration.

This has been going on for a long time, but I think this latest conversion will probably stick.

It took place at 8:15 A.M. in a Fred Harvey restaurant on the Tri-State toll road near Hinsdale, Illinois. It was a gray, misty, sunless day, and I was taking my rented car back to O'Hare airport after a five-day speaking tour of colleges in the Midwest.

I had stopped for breakfast in the Harvey restaurant. The mini-skirted waitress, straight out of teenland with false eyelashes and green mascaraed lids, had seated me at a window below which six lanes of frenzied traffic roared in and out of the underpass at 75 miles an hour. It was like being suspended above the Indianapolis Speedway during the running of the 500, only here the racers were going both ways. These tollway restaurants form monstrous overpasses that stretch like glassed-in bunkers across the obstacle course of blazing cars. Vehicles of every conceivable size, shape, and color sweep to and fro; 198 a minute by actual count, spewing in and out of the concrete underpass like missiles in a race for time. Plainly, on this murky morning, someone had pushed the panic button and America was off and running.

This was not the first time I had eaten in one of these dizzy disheries, but this morning certain features made me reflective. For one thing, when the long-haired waitress set a glass of water, a paper place mat and the plastic cutlery in front of me, I gave my automatic order: "Half a grapefruit, whole wheat toast, two boiled eggs," and then turned back immediately to the hypnotic stream of campers, tankers, tandems, semis, limos, vans, pickups, sports cars and coupes, bursting from the tunneled cannon's mouth and speeding unerringly between the barely visible skeins of white dividing lines.

To my left, this same wild purgatorial scene was heading south, while in the adjoining right lanes the projectory was northward, headlights blazing through the rising mist, iridescent beetles ramming the apertures at the speed of sound.

My head was still cocked over the pulsating speedway when I heard the waitress say, "Sir? Sir, we don't have boiled eggs."

"You don't?"

"We have eggs," she made clear.

"But not boiled eggs?"

"Right."

"It doesn't really matter," I said while the swish of the cars resounded like snaps of circus whips. "But why can't a person get boiled eggs?"

"Just a moment, I'll ask."

"No! Wait!"

She was off at a tempo matching the traffic below. North and south the vehicular rocket-fire drew me back in hopeless enchantment. Swissh! Zooomm! Shoosh! A Mayflower van chased the tail of its Bekins competitor. A Volkswagen sped between the awesome shadows of a Greyhound bus and a van marked Irvin Zink. A Honda with two helmeted riders cut a swath ahead of a Texaco tanker. A camper pulling a boat signaled a lane change, while a pickup loaded with kids and a yelping dog roared ahead of a horse trailer from which the filly's tail dangled in the wind.

The fog lifted. The variegated colors of the endless streams of flying cars bedeviled the eyes and stoned the mind. Bare inches quivered between steel and flying steel. Shades of Dante strode through my head and I caught myself saying,

> *Out from the underpass covered with dew,*
> *The torrent of traffic continued to spew.*

The sun came through to better unveil this automotive firing line and call attention to trucks and semis flicking by like symbols on a giant ticker tape: P.I.E., U-HAUL, HERTZ, SHELL, HENNIS, O.I.C., HILDE-BRAND, C.C.C., MAC, O.T.C., MIDAS.

These multi-sized dragons continued to belch forth out of the tunnel beneath me, as if determined there should be no rest and no end to this catenation even if it killed them. And I got to thinking that I, along with all the others, had been and would again be a part of it as soon as I had gulped down my meal

"Sir? Sir, they say they don't boil eggs because they don't have the equipment."

"It requires equipment?"

"I guess so. We do have eggs. Scrambled?"

"Scrambled," I agreed.

Her smile was sweet. I turned once more to gaze at the incredible panorama where only the blurred white lines protected the Kamikaze drivers and only the grace of God guarded the innocent.

Speaking of Him, I wondered what went on in His mind as He looked down night and day while the noxious fumes rose higher and thicker, staining His great white throne.

I was Dante looking down on hell's heat.

> *Coughing and watching, wide-eyed with dread,*
> *The God of creation was shaking His head.*

"Sir? Sir, your grapefruit."

"Thank you. Tell me, do you ever get used to it?"

"To what, sir?"

"Down there. The scramble."

"Oh, it goes on all the time. Harvey's never closes."

"Do you get used to it?"

"First few days it made me dizzy. Y'know? Really dizzy. And I felt like they were coming right at me. Right *into* me. Especially on the night shift. The lights. But I didn't get dizzy at night. During the day when I'd stand at the window, that's when I got dizzy. When I'd watch. Both ways. Y'know? No, it don't bother me any more. You get to feel like it wasn't there. I'll bring your eggs."

Looking down again, I felt very much a part of it. I saw myself manning the diesel truck spouting soot and steam. I could feel my muscles respond as I steered the canvas-covered cargo marked EXPLOSIVES. I was at the wheel of the sports car, the camper, the fuel tanker, the moving van. I was driving my rented car in and out of the underpass through rain and sleet and sun and shadow from dawn to dusk and dusk to dawn.

"Sir? Sir, you did say whole wheat toast? And the eggs—scrambled. There you are." She set them down and promised to be back.

What, I wondered, would happen if the interlacing flow of traffic all over the world slowed down to 35 miles an hour instead of the customary 70 and 75? What if the total tempo of life could be calmed down proportionately? It probably wouldn't be fun. There must be something about the chase, the pace, the maze, the daring, the competition, the escape that helps us prove something deep in the human psyche and drives us on. There is an illusion that we live *more* if we live faster. And if we die at three score years and ten, we have the satisfaction of having crowded six score years and twenty into life's package and gotten double our money's worth.

On the other hand, wasn't it possible that we would live longer—both in illusion and reality—if we lived slower? Certainly we would see more in *particular* if we slowed down, though we now see more in *general* because we are speeded up.

What bothered me was something more basic. I liked to be in a position where I could control the situation, but on the toll road of life I was being controlled. Someone was always behind me, pushing. Someone was always in front of me, daring me to pass. I learned long ago that you are fairly safe from arrest by a vigilant traffic cop if you keep moving with the flow of traffic and can prove you are a link in the endless chain. What was basically wrong with the world, I concluded, was that its rhythm was not of my making, its speed not of my doing, and many of its requirements not of my choosing. The hour had come for my conversion.

Meantime the roaring never let up for a moment, down to the final nibble at my whole wheat toast. The sun was now up and shining on a rush of GOODWILL INDUSTRIES, MARSHALL FIELD'S, U.S. MAIL, MOBIL, SEARS, EXPLOSIVES, FLAMMABLE! Now the bodies of the multi-colored cars were luminous, and occasionally a spattered bumper sticker splurted its message: AMERICA RIGHT OR WRONG; CARLS-BAD CAVERNS; MAKE LOVE NOT WAR; JESUS SAVES; WHERE WILL YOU SPEND ETERNITY?

"Sir? Sir, your check. Thank you very much. Have a good day."

I envied her. She was above it all. She would have told me with a shrug that, "This is the way it is. Y'know?" Sometimes it rains, sometimes the sun shines. Some places serve boiled eggs, some don't. Some people are fun, others aren't. Some days are okay, others are a drag.

That might all be very well for her, but I was making up my mind once and for all as I had done a hundred times before. For me the quiet life was the grand desideratum. This was the very last time I would travel the fury of the toll road. I would finish up this trip, drop my 30¢ into the last of the mechanized coin-catchers, wait for the automatic signal that said THANK YOU! and figure out the O'Hare interchange. Then I would turn in my rented car and lug my bags to the airline check-in, praying that my plane would be on time, the weather flyable, the connections workable, the stewardesses amiable, the food edible, and that my wife would have our car at the L.A. airport and welcome me home.

From here on, the rule would be quietude for me.

It was remarkable how it all worked out. When I got back into the toll road traffic the weather had completely cleared. The streams of flying cars flowed along so smoothly and with such kinetic timing that I was almost proud to be a link in the flawless forward movement. What a marvel is man to build these precision vehicles, to chart these highways and engineer these trails through industrial jungles and into the teeming city itself so that we can keep the needle steadily at 70 all the way! What an incredible network of lanes leading anywhere you wished to go! What master minds lay behind these intertwisting concrete puzzles, guiding me unerringly straight to the check-in office while the roar of planes thundered overhead and the streak of jets carved their contrails in the sky!

Sooner than I had dared hope, I was taking off in a luxury liner, on time, sun shining, engines musically churning, stewardesses smiling. Another moment and I was looking down on it all, the city, the landscape, the homes, the streets, the traffic, the horizon rimmed with fluffs of clouds stretching out into the spaceless sea of blue.

I reclined my cushioned seat and relaxed. What a lovely world! What a life! What a magical place is mother earth and what a wonderland she has provided for us in which to do our thing, work out our dreams, and play our little game of life!

I closed my eyes and visualized the scene waiting for me at the L.A. International. My wife would be there with her enthusiastic welcome. Our schnauzer would be waiting in the car, greeting me as if I had been away forever. We would wait our turn and pay our parking fee and in the next moment become part of the freeway traffic in the West Coast's most imposing megalopolis.

And so it was. As we sped through the freeway lanes at 75 under sunny skies a bit besmirched with smog, with cars flanking us on every side, my wife said, "Well, how was it? How was the trip?"

"Great," I said, as I had done on endless homecomings of this kind. "Real great."

And in the morning when we sat in our breakfast nook (where I finally got my boiled eggs), at a window looking out on camellia blossoms, a magnolia tree and birds feeding in the grass, it all looked new and fresh —somehow even more poignantly so because of the toll road that runs, one way or another, through every life.

.18.

The Summary

After the analogies, allegories and romantic rational, what's *really* right with the world when viewed realistically in the light of our time? It is all very well to concentrate on the micro-world of self and find some separate, specific good. But what about the macro-world, the power world, the dog-eat-dog world, the multimedia world from which there is no reasonable escape? Must we ignore the world around us in order to find something truly right about it?

We can't ignore it even if we want to, but we can interpenetrate it. That is the point when all is said and done—and that, of course, is my main theme, all the way from "The Bridle Path" to "The Toll Road." The best way to deal with complexities and dilemmas is to view the macro-world from within the framework of a balanced micro-world until the outward vision can be gauged and governed by a sound inward sight. Develop a sturdy in-world where you are in control, where you see things from your highest perspective. Without this, the power world dehumanizes and depersonalizes even the best of us.

"Sure," says sociologist Hall Sprague, who left La Jolla Behavorial Sciences Institute to "find himself," "sure, we can talk about more things these days, but something in our soul withers, and those sense organs that used to be so important to our survival and joy are deadened. We are less like our special brand of animal life, less viscerally spirited, less confident of our ability to cope successfully with a physical environment. What to do? Periodically, I stop watching TV, ignore the papers, pass up the jazzy magazine covers, leave the car radio off. At first there is a feeling of deprivation, but after a while, it is nice. I get inklings of the 'in person' man inside me. I notice flowers, weeds, birds, trees, noises, sounds, smells, textures. My mind still spins at times, but it rotates around more immediate problems which might yield to interventions I can make unassisted."

Sprague went from the macro-world to the micro-world to find what was right with himself. I went from the micro-world to the macro-world to discover what's right with the latter. The odyssey runs both ways, and both are right and good. Either way, a clearer inner vision helps us see through the smudge and maya of things with the chance of catching, through psychic sight, what William Blake envisioned when he said, "If the doors of perception were cleansed, everything would appear to man as it really is, infinite."

What's right with the world? A number of things. First of all, there is a definite rightness in the fact that *the overall trend these days is from exclusiveness to inclusiveness* in our micro-thinking no less than in many of our macro-ways. I tried to interpret this by way of "The Bridle Path." Athlete or handicapped, it makes no difference; the modern phenomenon of this rightness goes beyond any outward appearance or social or psychological differences. Individuals, whoever or whatever they are, are equal parts of the human race. Each is essential in his own right, necessary in the yin-yang equation, filling a place, serving a need, telling us something about ourselves and our own longing for fulfillment.

The spastic's courageous rise out of the dust of the bridle path, no less than the eloquent stride of the jogger, reaches out beyond the limits of the sheltered path and has something to say to everyone, no matter what his situation, his equipment, or his state of being. Here is something deeply reasoned and deeply felt, and but for this near-home happening I might never have closed a gap in my viewpoint when I looked out across the world. I would still have seen only the apparent injustices between seemingly favored and unfavored individuals. This closer insight got the haunted thought of inequities out of my mind and made me realize that tracks in the sand, my own included, are both permanent and impermanent in the historic flow of life.

"The Singing" supported the same view, the assurance that we are moving from exclusiveness to inclusiveness in our personal and social evaluations. I was in the U.S.S.R. long before an American president journeyed there. I was there in the days when it would have been inconceivable to imagine such a summit visitation in view of the prejudices our two governments fostered and imposed upon their people. Instead of accepting and explaining how alike our deep-seated aspirations actually were, both sides promoted suspicion, stirred up animosities and made sure that an iron curtain remained as vivid as the wall.

We were as exclusive as they, but there came a time when a new approach surfaced, an approach long held in the consciousness of those who had consistently doubted the superiority of one nation over another. Christmas in Kharkov *was* like Christmas in my Wisconsin town. The luminescent white of the snow piling on lamps, wires, trees and city streets revealed the fiction of divided worlds long before political bridges were built. Seen through the eyes of the "average man," nature's wonderland and an inner feeling were sufficiently real and compelling to persuade him there is something right in the universal response to such a time and place.

I heard the words "America is our Christian neighbor" from the common people long before the phrase was ever believed, before we even dared talk about it for fear of being misunderstood. But they knew and we knew that faith makes no distinction between those who truly worship, no matter where or how or what form their worship takes. Whatever strange new twist a future fate may take, at the moment, across the land and throughout the globe, the trend from exclusiveness to inclusiveness suggests there is something conceivably right at work in the world.

"The Slogan" also epitomized this trend. When I recall that the Hutterian people were once considered a group of fanatical utopian experimenters, cutting themselves off from society, living behind the taut barbed wire of their communes, shut off from a culture they did not know and which did not know them except by way of preconceptions, it is phenomenal that young America has found in them a symbol of something they felt had been lost in the way of oneness with the land and family life.

It was a small event, to be sure, that the Hutterites, who rarely leave the commune, visited us on our home ground. But the songs they sang and the things they said reached far beyond the lake front and the nearby hills. The longing for love and understanding that we felt was symptomatic of the coming together of races and cultures in many similar intimate and unpublicized gatherings. What we were experiencing in our micro-world was definitely an indication of a universal hunger for fellowship and honest identification in the world at large.

This particular rightness, the move from exclusiveness to inclusiveness, was fronted by a second significant trend among us worldlings: *the shift from a sense of infallibility to an attitude of honest evaluation of what we actually believe in enough to live by.* In the light of my research, this phenomenon looms as a spectacular transition. When I began my study of religious groups some thirty years ago, sectarian walls were so rigid and unyielding that an orthodox Protestant would have thought twice about walking on the Catholic side of the street, and no self-respecting Catholic cleric would have stepped inside a Protestant sanctuary even out of curiosity. As for the crossing of Christian and non-Christian lines, there were no passageways. The denominational world was divided into camps of doctrinal infallibility. History's bloodiest wars were "religious," from the ancient Thirty Years' War between Catholics and Protestants to the apocalyptic overtones of the incredibly long conflict in Vietnam. To be infallible, generalissimos had God on their side, and this had been accepted from the time of Constantine straight through to Hirohito. All was part of an historic tradition, but the expansion of a new spiritual insight was moving through the ranks of the people. Infallibility was metamorphizing into a quest for peace, and there was growing evidence of a deep-seated search for alternatives based on new aspects of spiritual understanding.

"The Chrysalis" had this viewpoint in mind. It tried to say that the best way to make these transitional moments graphic *is* to allegorize them. Factualism is not enough. We recognize and accept change in the macro-world only if we can relate it to an experience within ourselves. We are convinced of it when we are part of the phenomenon.

Hence, histolysis. Here was something we had ob-served in our own backyard, or had felt within ourselves when we remembered some of the revolutionary changes that had taken place in us. At any rate, I felt it was easier to relate to the caterpillar and the birth of a butterfly when thinking about a rebirth in conscious-ness, or even life after death for that matter, than to accept these hypotheses on the basis of theology. If the unconscious *is* the chrysalis in which new awarenesses are born and new worlds and new insights fashioned, then this is remarkably right. Consciousness in each of us is a controllable world.

"The Bridge" underscored this trend toward honest evaluation as we observe it in the scientific and meta-physical fields. Today there are no longer any phenom-ena too far out or too isolated for serious investigation. Hypnotism, which evolved from a vaudevillian stunt into an accredited therapy, was a case in point. One breakthrough triggers another. Conscientious research quietly tests the claim of infallibility in field after field. One by one, age-old beliefs are probed, and the logical answer to the complaint that "nothing is sacred" is that most sacred of all is the quest for truth and understand-ing of universal law.

Recently the Astronomy Survey Committee of the National Academy of Sciences reported on the possibil-ity of life beyond earth in terms that would have been considered totally irrational a few short years ago. The report referred to the strange celestial objects called quasars and pulsars. It urged a new program costing $300 million a year in the field of detection of intelligent "life out there." Said the report, "Our civilization is within reach of one of the greatest steps in evolution: knowledge of the possible nature and existence of independent civilizations in space. At this instant, through this very document, are perhaps passing radio waves bearing the conversations of distant creatures, conversations which we could record if we but pointed a radio telescope in the right direction and tuned in on the proper frequency."

In the days of "The Bridge" this would have been considered as heretical as Galileo's insistence on the experimental method and his own position against infallibility, but today this 17th-century physicist would finally have come into his own. Surely open-mindedness is a step toward rightness in a world where the earth is truly, as he contended, systematically revolving around the sun, though once he stood alone in his belief and was condemned for his contention.

"The Dreaming" touched another tangent of the trend toward honest evaluation and a sense of give and take. I remember my first research trip some thirty years ago among the Doukhobors in Canada and the Voodooists in Haiti. I was told there was nothing valid that could be learned from either sect. In those days scientists refused to examine isolated phenomena, and sociologists disdained to look for signs of development of modes of thought which might lead from the magical to the religious and on into the scientific. Nor had anthropologists begun to synthesize the wide range of ethnic and cultural information. It was of a breakaway from this parochial outlook that "The Dreaming" tried to tell. Here was a time in aboriginal culture when individuals gave themselves a chance for idealistic imagining, utopian longing, of the kind we sophisticated moderns reach for in our meditative rituals whatever they may be or whatever form they take.

Even "The Kennel" was a case in point, an argument against the ropes and knots of "no escape" from authoritarian infallibility. Celsus was actually his name. No fiction here. No fiction about any part of the story, or any of the other stories for that matter. These things happen, as every writer knows. They are fed into his mill. They materialize. Celsus was his name and he was doomed for a box if he wished to fly. But he was also *Para*celsus, and he had the truth built into him which those best understand who catch on to the secret of living in harmony with their world.

This led to a third basic rightness which can best be stated as *a turn from a disregard of nature to a respect for nature and her laws.* There is more involved here than an emphasis on ecological factors. In fact, we can never truly effect a sincere ecological breakthrough without a sense of personal involvement with the total natural resources of planet Earth, so much so that a most wonderful rightness with the world is a growing awareness of oneness with our environment, with animal life, with the land and forests, with vegetation, water, air and earth; a new love and attitude toward nature; a nature consciousness expressed in "The Gloria Patri," "The Swallows," "The Gannets," and even in "The Raft."

Such experiences may not be recorded in books on ecotactics or found in the literature of the Sierra Clubs, but they are of the life stuff that builds the foundation for interterrestrial relationships and cooperative commitment to our environmental world. A short generation ago, the very word ecology was practically unknown, as was ecumenism, and both have a great deal in common when considered in the context of respect for the innate qualities of man and nature's world. We now realize that they have been inextricably bound together from the earliest days when man's faith was animistic and his church and altars were formations nature had made for him in the hills and groves and streams of God's great out-of-doors.

It is one thing to be told that we must clear up the environment and be co-workers in the future of the ecosystem, to be cajoled into emulating Smokey the Bear or warned by pronouncements of governments and corporations that the idyllic world is up to us. It is quite another approach to so love the interplay of living things that a reverence for all life becomes a natural basis for our acts.

Sadie's song is another example of the third basic rightness. As I have said, all I ever knew about sandpipers was that they said "Beep-beep," and that they teetered. But this was only because I had never seen them in their moment of creation when, for a little while, they sang their secret songs. There is a lesson in this having to do with our relationship not only to birds but to the total family of mankind as well. And that is the philosophy being born in this shift from a disregard of nature to a respect for nature and her laws.

There is something so beautifully and profoundly right about a world like this—and something doubly right to think we are a living part of it. Penelope O'Hare, in her transformation from self-centeredness to a kinship with other lives, is an example of the growing sensitivity I constantly find among the younger-than Penelope, counter-culture generations. I saw these young people at work in the endless clean-up job following the Santa Barbara oil spills. I knew the motivation behind their tireless work in fighting the brush fires in the Los Angeles area. The world is presenting them with a new challenge—to undo what less aware members of their own generation and older generations did before them, and to do it with a mystic, pantheistic view not always understood.

Sometimes, as I sat with them, their talk sounded like a put-on as they expressed their feeling for the ancient Norsemen who never felled a tree without planting another in its place, or romanced about the Druids who in their veneration pruned the oak groves only with a silver sickle, or the Japanese farmer who planted and harvested his rice with the prayer that he might be a good custodian of his fields, or the Aardvark who knew he was more dependent upon animal life than the animals were dependent on him. Sharing their aphorisms, they reminded me that, "The early farmers of the British Commonwealth had a motto, 'Live as though you were to die tomorrow, but farm as though you were to live forever,' " and "The American Indian, he never took more than he needed."

Listening to them and sharing with them some of their so-called equinoctial festivals, I was moved, as in the case of Penelope, by memories of my own ardent youth. Echoes reverberating in me asked, "What have I lost? Can I blame it on the world? Is it really the fault of others?"

Or, as "The Raft" reported: The adventurers on their "chip" in the swinging sea, and Whittaker on his, Alvin on his, I on mine and the millions of our contemporaries who make up the current passenger list—we are all in the same boat, and there is a reasoned rightness in the recognition of our oneness with the universe as we steer a new and thrilling course that keeps both nature and ourselves in mind.

All of which brought into focus a fourth important point: *A fundamental rightness about the world is that it is constantly bringing into being the coming of a new, unique individual, the balanced micro-macro person* of the kind depicted philosophically in "The Carousel," psychologically in "The Unforgettable," sociologically in "The Lens," patriotically in "The American," and scientifically in "The 747." That was the idea, a way of saying that this universal person is unfettered in his search for truths to live by, taking both ancient wisdom and honest modern thought—symbolism, imagery and mythology, no less than the latest, tested technological achievement—subliminally into his inner consciousness. More interested in existence than in things that exist, he is ready to admit that the answer to his deepest quest is found within the quest itself.

That was why the protagonist in "The Carousel," though on crutches, walked more vigorously, philosophically, than many another stronger player in life's scene. He had the micro-macro balance that made him say, "I'll tell you what's right with the world: friends, taxi drivers, waitresses, a guide dog, champions, moments, letters, nature, quarrels." Such was his world. He was convinced of it, and that is why I still see him swinging himself trustfully through his garden where the flowers bloomed.

That, too, is why "The Unforgettable" taught me that we can better meet the rush and pace of things by returning to moments of remembered calm. We can endure loneliness by recalling the hours when we wished with all our heart that we could be alone. Memory keeps weaving in and out of our day-by-day encounters, balancing our lives, helping us keep our bearings, steadying our sense of values, giving us the grand connection with the infinite and eternal as if we were actually in control—which we usually are, especially if we remember that the epicenter of our micro-world is our source of power and that our macro-world is steady and secure because of it. Again, we create a new consciousness in the universe around us only by developing new attitudes within ourselves. As the Jamesian axiom puts it, "We cannot correct corrupt conditions unless we are strong enough not to be corrupted by the conditions we wish to correct."

The emerging micro-macro man no longer thinks of the world "out there" as being beyond his influence. The putting off of the "old" man and putting on the "new" is an adventure simultaneously involving individuation and society, an experience beyond words, communicating between generations on a non-verbal, subliminal basis.

Recently, in a symposium, it was suggested we make a distinction between that which is *complex* and that which is *complicated.* When we say a problem is complex, we mean that the organism or the situation is orderly but we do not quite understand it. Nonetheless, there is an inherent pattern. When we designate a thing as complicated, we imply that there is no discernible pattern. Is it possible that those of the once so-called establishment often look upon life and society as being complex, while emerging generations consider them as complicated? Perhaps if we could communicate against the background of this sort of understanding and then remember the importance of non-verbal communication, the language of things felt and values truly believed, the rightness of the world in our particular time in history would become more clear.

"The American" suggests that complexities and complications, inner and outer worlds, will and the deed are complementary, reciprocal, unitive as in the yin-yang, principle of which is *duality in such harmonious relationship that duality appears monistic.*

The recognition of this interplay is the life-style of the new individual and constitutes an obvious rightness in our world. H. J. B. was cited as a homespun example of one whose healthy approach to life rests on the knowledge of the full range of other people's thoughts and aspirations, respects them and quietly assimilates them into her own creative sphere.

Since it is freedom that provides the best soil for the growth of this new being, America is challenged to be his rightful home, but with the ancestral proviso that the better the American, the more truly is he a citizen of the world; even as the emerging new individual recognizes that the deeper and more meaningful his own personal faith, the greater are his respect and understanding of the living faiths of all mankind. Such is the power of perception and the paradox of spiritual understanding of the life in our time.

This is the message of "The Toll Road" a lapse into anecdote and a slice of life from the experience of every man who ever ventured off the open road. It was there, as I said, that I wondered what would happen if the interlacing flow of traffic all around the globe slowed down to thirty-five miles an hour and the total tempo of life could be calmed down proportionately. I felt that we probably wouldn't enjoy it. We would miss whatever it is about the fast pace, the high adventure, the competition, that satisfies something deep within us and drives us on. But although we feel that by living faster we live more, isn't it possible that we would live longer both in illusion and in reality if we lived at a slower pace? And isn't it true that we would see more things in greater detail if we slowed down?

I used to speculate that what was basically wrong with the world was that its rhythm was not of my making, its speed not of my doing, and many of its requirements and demands not of my choosing. But always there was my inner, micro-world, played upon, sharpened and inspired by this macro-world which others seemingly had made. The more I discussed this with those "others" the more I realized that they felt as I did, both about the annoyances and about the thrill of traveling on the toll road at such a time in history and in our own lives!

Perhaps, I concluded, all we need do is make this sense of something right collective, bring it into unification, so that in time, through each one of us as an emissary, we will discover rightness in other hearts and eventually recognize that micro- and macro-world are both basically in *us* and constitute a state of consciousness inseparable, indivisible, universal—the dynamism of life itself.

We already have that better world without quite realizing it. And that may be the one thing wrong with our relationship with the world at large. We are afraid to admit how right it really is or to confess how reluctant we are to give up this world even for a promised land which is supposed to be considerably more idyllic than the exciting one we reflectively refer to as the Earth, our home.